Writing America

Writing America

CLASSROOM LITERACY AND PUBLIC ENGAGEMENT

EDITED BY

Sarah Robbins and Mimi Dyer

FOREWORD BY **Paul Lauter**

Teachers College, Columbia University
New York and London

National Writing Project
Berkeley, California

Published simultaneously by Teachers College Press, 1234 Amsterdam Avenue, New York, NY 10027 and the National Writing Project, 2105 Bancroft Way, Berkeley, CA 94720-1042.

Library of Congress Cataloging-in-Publication Data

Writing America : classroom literacy and public engagement / edited by Sarah Robbins and Mimi Dyer ; foreword by Paul Lauter.
    p. cm.
  Includes bibliographical references and index.
  ISBN 0-8077-4527-8 (pbk. : alk. paper)
    1. United States—History, Local—Study and teaching. 2. Community life—Study and teaching—United States. I. Robbins, Sarah. II. Dyer, Mimi. III. National Writing Project (U.S.)

E180.W75 2005
307'.071'073—dc22   2004053731

ISBN 0-8077-4527-8 (paper)

Printed on acid-free paper
Manufactured in the United States of America

12 11 10 09 08 07 06 05   8 7 6 5 4 3 2 1

Contents

 Foreword

What should schools do? Generally that question is answered in terms of what the society expects schools to do *for*—or more accurately, perhaps, *to*—individual students: socialize them; track them into jobs, college, the army, marriage, or even jail; provide them with one or another marketable skill; familiarize them with the myths and images that are supposed to express our values. Too seldom do we focus on the question of what schools should do in their role as community institutions.

Of course, we know schools as places in which adults meet, vote, perhaps take a night course. But more than that, as community institutions, schools carry out the two tasks explicit in the name of the project from which this book has emerged: Keeping and Creating American Communities. "Keeping," because even in schools' names; in the historical memory represented by their teachers, alumni, students, and parents; in the myriad ways nationally produced textbooks and curricula are locally implemented; in their own histories; and in the very street names, now disused, chiseled into the cornerstone of the elementary school across from where I write, schools are major resources in sustaining community here in America and throughout the world. No wonder they are so conflicted. Schools enact the saying "Think globally, act locally." And in so doing, they "keep," sustain, whatever it is we mean by community.

But "community" is no static phenomenon, nor are schools archives. Communities are forever being *created* and re-created. And particularly by those who engage one another in, around, and sometimes, alas, in spite of our schools. It is here that generations cross, that they come together to interpret and reinterpret what has been, may now be, or might become curious, interesting, even vital to life together on this crowded planet. It is from here, as these essays show, that teachers and students can reach out to create the meanings we designate as "heritage," "neighborhood," "history"—knowledge, in short. In that process, teachers and students answer the persistent question at the heart of intellectual life: Why this, in this way, at this time, in this place?

To think about schools as institutions for "keeping and creating" community is to think differently about education itself. One moves away, to use Sarah Robbins's image, from "prescribed roadways" to unexplored pathways of "authentic inquiry." For the localities in which schools work are always distinctive: Understanding, sustaining, creating local communities will thus involve distinctive acts of imagination and inquiry. It is here in particular that these essays provide models for teachers, students, and others interested in education and community, as distinct from test scores and political sound bites. For these are essays rooted in the difficult practice of drawing students out by drawing them into the wonderful projects these teachers have developed and shared with us.

In this educational context, too, expressing what one discovers becomes not a mechanical form of what's called *literacy*, but an act of social engagement. We write, we photograph, we display, not so much to satisfy standardized expectations—though we likely do that better—as to communicate our discoveries, our stories, and our visions of the communities we share to those with whom we would speak. Engagement and expression become the standards, rather than standardization the measure of achievement.

What should schools do? Educate, of course. And these essays offer not prescriptions but insights about how what is meant by *education* and what is meant by *community* come together with excitement and mutually sustaining power.

—Paul Lauter

Acknowledgments

Growing out of a project focused on community interactions, this book naturally has many debts to individuals and groups far beyond our list of chapter authors. First, we thank the National Endowment for the Humanities (NEH) and the National Writing Project (NWP). While funding from these two organizations has been crucial to the Keeping and Creating American Communities (KCAC) program, the personal support of mentors in the NEH and the NWP has been even more important. In particular, we thank our program officers at the NEH, Janet Edwards and Robert Sayers, and the many NWP site directors and national leaders who provided ongoing advice and who continually signaled their belief in our program. We especially appreciate the involvement of NWP leaders Joye Alberts, Robert Brooke, Elyse Eidman-Aadahl, and Amy Bauman. Our "pilot teachers" from other NWP sites—Judy Bebelaar from the Bay Area Writing Project, Barbara Howry from the Oklahoma Writing Project, and Sharon Bishop from the Nebraska Writing Project—will surely see the influence of their KCAC participation in these pages. Most of all, from among our NWP colleagues, we thank the Red Cedar Writing Project's Diana Mitchell, who served with great energy and commitment on our KCAC National Advisory Board.

All the meetings of our board were hosted by the American Studies Association (ASA) during the ASA's annual fall conference. But the ASA's involvement in this project went well beyond such material resources. Most of our advisory board members are ASA members, and the ASA annual conventions served as a major venue for the first dissemination of our work in sessions where attendees gave supportive suggestions that are now reflected in this book. We especially thank the ASA-affiliated members of our National Advisory Board: Randy Bass, Thadious Davis, Cristine Levenduski, Paul Lauter, and David Scobey.

Besides colleagues from the organizations named above, we thank the many members of local groups (such as historical societies, PTAs, and local corporate sponsors)—as well as individual community members—who have graciously given resources to our work. Special thanks go to Taronda Spencer, archivist at the Spelman College Library, and Professor Dana White of Emory University for their support of our research. We also appreciate the contributions of fellow teachers who joined us in various classroom projects, as well as administrators who provided time for us to meet as a project community, encouraged our curricular experiments, and supported the writing of our individual chapters in a variety of ways.

Not everyone on the KCAC participant team has chosen to write an essay for this collection. Everyone who participated in the program has contributed substantially to the content of this book, however, because all of us involved in the KCAC initiative constantly traded ideas and reformed our classroom practices collaboratively. Different team members focused on different avenues for disseminating what they learned—for example, organizing workshops for teachers or preparing materials for our project Web site—while contributing informally to other publication venues. We thank the entire KCAC community for helping bring these particular stories to more public life in print.

In preparing this book, we received expert support from Teachers College Press editor Carol Collins and other TCP staff members. Particularly helpful were the anonymous reviews of our manuscript that we received early in the publication process. Thanks also to support staff, student assistants, and interns from the Kennesaw State University Department of English for their assistance with many editorial tasks. Special thanks go to the Kennesaw Mountain Writing Project's program coordinator, Stacie Janecki, for her tireless work on permissions and manuscript preparation.

We are grateful to the many students whose classroom work is chronicled here. We also thank the generous colleagues who facilitated sessions during summer institutes and school-year seminars for the KCAC program.

To learn more about the KCAC project, we hope readers will visit our Web site at http://kcac.kennesaw.edu, where additional writing by many more KCAC teachers provides supplementary resources for hands-on classroom use and materials that would be helpful to anyone planning similar professional development projects for educators.

PROLOGUE

Keeping and Creating Teachers' Learning Communities

Elyse Eidman-Aadahl

In her introduction to the Keeping and Creating American Communities (KCAP) project (Chapter 1), Sarah Robbins describes the KCAC program as inviting teachers and students to see themselves both as cultural stewards and as cultural creators, active composers of a community identity. The essays in this volume demonstrate the vitality of this twinned identity not only for powerful classrooms and curricula, but also for communities hungry for connections to schools and young people. But these essays also reflect the keeping and creating of another community—the professional community of the Kennesaw Mountain Writing Project (KMWP), a National Writing Project (NWP) site since 1994. Indeed, it is by doing work together in just this way that teachers bring a writing project into being and continue its traditions.

As director of national programs and site development for the NWP, I have been a friend to the KMWP and interested observer of KCAC over many years. I've had the pleasure of watching the work of these committed and talented educators unfold over time. From the vantage point of the NWP and its network of more than 185 sites across the country, KCAC provides a window into a local writing project creating itself as a community of practice. Now 30 years old, the NWP has been described in publications as diverse as *Teachers at the Center*, the personal memoir of founder James Gray (2000), and *Inside the National Writing Project*, a study by Ann Lieberman and Diane Wood (2002) of the NWP as a professional development network. Publications such as these aim to detail the values, core practices, and ways of working that characterize the NWP approach to professional development. In this book we glean insights into how teachers and scholars committed to these values, practices, and approaches take on new challenges and create new opportunities for their own professional development. To the degree that KCAC created conditions for what Cris Levenduski describes as "the best of what we hope might happen daily in our schools," we would do well to understand these teachers as founders and stewards of teachers' ongoing learning communities.

The key is in *ongoing*. It is hard to imagine calling something *a community* if it holds no view of its own continuation. The temporary community created by travelers on a train, strangers in a waiting room, or even teachers in a summer course rarely produces a sense of collective ambition or mutual futures. A community holds its future as open ended, not finite. Local writing-project sites, like subject matter projects and teacher networks, are similarly intended to be open-ended, long-term enterprises, designed and led by teachers for teachers. Although their offices and some activities will be housed at colleges and universities and supported by a variety of local and national partners, the community exists in the work teachers imagine to do together, the routines and rituals of reflection and teacher research, the practices of making teaching and curriculum public, and the habits of inquiry and response that mark the writing project. A writing project is therefore less a place or a course than something teachers choose to do together. What, then, are some of the features of the community, of the work that KMWP teachers chose to do together in creating and sustaining KCAC?

CREATING TEACHERS' LEARNING COMMUNITIES

Vital learning communities for teachers might be sparked or launched in a number of ways, but they won't survive long if they are not at base created and embraced by teachers. As Robbins describes in Chapter 1, KCAC was built on the shoulders of teacher-led curriculum projects in the NWP and elsewhere, sparked by a wide set of ideas and interests. But it was shaped by teacher leadership at all levels, right from the start. Not simply an effort designed in the university and offered to teachers or a set of resources sent to the local professional library, KCAC involved teachers in the design process, asked them to assume roles in management and assessment, and looked to them to lead major dissemination activities.

Teacher leadership has a practical side. Teacher-leaders were responsible for important design decisions, decisions that shaped the project effectively to the occupational lives and culture of the participants. Teachers also extended the base capacity of the project to make and do work. But for KCAC, as for local writing projects, teacher leadership has an even more important rationale: It signals the assumption that all participants are capable of important intellectual work and hold common responsibility for creating powerful learning environments for themselves and their peers. Leadership that is explicitly linked to our work as teachers, curriculum makers, and scholars creates delicious ambitions: ambitions for the work of the classroom to extend beyond the classroom, beyond the walls of the school, and beyond the ephemeral moment of the lesson. Those ambitions, not for ourselves but for the power of our ideas and the potential of what we might be creating, fuel teachers' learning communities and are evident throughout these essays. Also evident is how KCAC teachers carried these assumptions and expectations over to their teaching, viewing students and community partners as capable of important intellectual work and inviting them to form grand ambitions, too.

When teachers lead, what kind of work do they design? In KCAC, the work that teachers and scholars created together was shaped by teachers' own questions and intellectual interests. While the project offered rich disciplinary frames, new resources, and powerful conceptual tools, its core assumption was that teachers would work with, extend, and adapt these to their own purposes as educators. In KCAC, teachers were never instrumentalized as conduits for knowledge made elsewhere to be distributed to our nation's schools. They were judged not by their fidelity to a script but for the rigor of their ideas and for their intellectual honesty. From the standpoint of the teacher committed to a line of inquiry, programs such as KCAC feel less like "outreach programs" than "in-reach programs": projects that allow teachers to "reach in" to the resources, ideas, perspectives, colleagueship of universities, scholars, and museums, without setting their identity as teachers aside. While it is certainly true that these teacher-scholars were "working for KCAC," creating an impressive array of curriculum resources, lesson plans, and pedagogical innovations, it was also true that KCAC was "working for them" by providing the resources and support to pursue their most powerful visions for their own classrooms. It is small wonder that KCAC teachers discovered approaches that would engage students, projects in which students work hard in classrooms and communities because their classrooms are working for them.

In-reach programs, of course, don't just happen because museums or libraries or university buildings unlock their doors. Key leaders—such as KMWP director Sarah Robbins, KCAC codirector Mimi Dyer, and the project's various "team leaders"—play vital roles in brokering access to networks of scholars, or in finding the right resource to match a current need, or in ensuring that all members of the community find the right kind of critical response to work in progress. It is therefore not surprising that the learning opportunities teachers create for themselves draw their vitality from the talents and inspiration of their local leaders rather than from distant policy pronouncements or needs assessments. Local leaders, of course, also look for ways to keep the vision and the knowledge of the community open so that their skills and talents help build the foundation, not the ceiling. Advisors, activities, and other opportunities are expected to open up new lines of inquiry, and everyone—including the project's advisors—are expected to view the resulting work as work in progress whose conclusion is open, not finite. It is small wonder that participating teachers found new models for teaching itself, models that centered on responding to students' inquiries and visions, brokering access, responding with critical encouragement, and articulating visions.

THE WORK OF THE COMMUNITY

Even when teachers' learning communities are launched through powerful visions and supported by key partners and leaders, they still must engage in work. They may, indeed, succeed or fail on the strength of the work they envision for themselves. As in any community, members can vote with their feet: It takes powerful and relevant work to hold a learning community together.

What does KCAC teach us about the work that sustains teachers' learning communities? Significantly, KCAC participants were given the time and resources, even the requirement, to "do the discipline" itself and to conduct their own primary research into community life and reflect on the experience. Throughout the essays we see the impact of teachers' beginning as learners and scholars themselves. By working in inquiry teams, conducting their own research, following the twists and turns in a project, offering up conclusions and constructions for public scrutiny, they became in some senses insiders to the knowledge they would teach. Having rich learning experiences with the material that teachers will use in their classrooms does more than provide example lessons or approaches to curriculum, though it may often do that. Working as leaders ourselves allows us to cultivate the habits and dispositions that infuse an area of study. It teaches us productive questions and active stances toward the material; it gives us the depth needed to coach and mentor our students through their own engagement with the material.

But most obviously, we see that KCAC was ultimately constructed in relationship to teachers' practice. Participating in KCAC, although time-consuming in many ways, more often deepened than detracted from the classroom. As Robbins describes the successive phases of KCAC, the overall arc of teacher research formed an organizing structure for the work. The stuff of classrooms and curriculum, the work of students, and the worlds of teachers' individual inquiry within a larger set of ideas and collegial relationships were as much a part of this project's design and reflection as the tools and frameworks of American studies, and each was made more significant in relation to the other. The core work of KCAC, as in many learning communities that teachers create for themselves, is to engage deeply with the work we do as teachers, to endow it with meaning and importance, to treat it as a subject with intellectual as well as practical interest. To do so, we learn to make the private worlds of classrooms public, first to our colleagues, then in larger and larger venues. It is small wonder that having done this, these teachers were able to create classrooms where students learned to similarly endow the local and the familiar with meaning and importance, to give its study serious attention, and to make their work public, too.

The practices of doing the discipline or engaging in the "real stuff" on the one hand, and, on the other, looking deeply at practice are common work in teachers' learning communities, but the doing and the application tend to feel incredibly specific. When really engaged with something important and specific, teachers in many learning communities come to see their colleagues as essential to their learning and growth. Who better than colleagues to understand what we are trying to accomplish in our teaching? Who else would be better positioned to push our thinking, to provide honest assessments of our work, to know just the right piece to read or person to connect to? For classroom teachers, who typically work in isolation from one another, the experience of intellectual fellowship and joint work is novel and powerful. This too has impact. Ironically, we isolated teaching professionals typically preside over groups. How will our classrooms change when we understand from the inside how knowledge is created in community?

KEEPING AS WELL AS CREATING TEACHERS' LEARNING COMMUNITIES

It is certainly possible to design professional development opportunities for teachers by creating the equivalent of the temporary community of travelers on a train, bonded together for a finite period, dispersing at the end, holding no vision of a common future. These opportunities have their place. But the teacher-scholars of KCAC conceived and enacted their work within the KMWP—a learning community with an open-ended future. In doing so, they were also preserving and sustaining a vision of teachers as learners, as colleagues, as leaders, and in their way as public intellectuals. This tradition, which animated teacher study groups and progressive professional associations of the past, is still at work in subject matter collaboratives and teacher networks today. This is a vision of the teaching profession particularly well suited to our higher ambitions for public education as a social good in a democracy. But both visions, of teaching and of public education, require active preservation lest they become buried memories, ideas with an "absence of presence."

As Robbins writes, KCAC teachers took seriously the NWP tenet that teachers of writing must write. Through writing, they created and preserved their community; this book is one result. But the call to writing is also our way of doing work together and, through work, creating our learning communities.

In the routines and rituals of writing project life, everyone pauses frequently to write, cast a few ideas into a notebook, test some language out on a colleague, listen while others do the same, searching together for an idea or image that seems to open the way to some new insight. Activities are built on the assumption that almost everyone present is likely involved in some inquiry into teaching or curriculum—whether we know it or not—and that knowledge is always provisional and open to critique, whether we like it or not. In the most everyday and mundane ways, the community reflects the expectation that anyone/everyone present is contributing to the shared knowledge of the community and that any one of our informal jottings might eventually become something quite serious indeed.

Many teachers coming to a writing project for the first time remark that they haven't been asked to write since college or since their most recent graduate course. Their observation points to the power of assignments and requirements and deadlines to motivate us to take on the hard work of generating and refining knowledge through writing. But it also reflects the occupational conditions of K–12 teaching with its emphasis on talk and performance, the scarcity of time for reflection, and the expectation that someone else (scholars and researchers?) makes knowledge while K–12 teachers merely distribute it. For teachers in much of the country, the effects of prescriptive teaching strategies, the narrowing of curriculum to match high-stakes assessments, and the creeping worry that our classrooms are merely the sum of our indices and rankings limit our collective sense of possibility. In contrast, the simple and unremarkable assumption that teachers are themselves writers, researchers, and knowledge makers feels revolutionary. We become hungry for the spirit of engagement and inquiry we experience at our writing project; we strive to re-create it in our classrooms and continue it through more joint work. Pretty soon, if all goes well, we begin to see our classrooms, our students, and our profession as full of possibility, particularly the mundane and routine possibility that virtually anyone (teacher, student, administrator, community member) might come up with something very smart, deeply insightful, positively witty, or irritatingly right.

The essays in this volume demonstrate the engagement, the spirit of inquiry, and the delicious ambition that results from taking the role of the teacher as public intellectual very seriously. For these teachers, authority/authoring come not from having successfully followed a set of scripted moves or from external rewards, but from having taken on real intellectual work with their students with all the challenges and potential associated with it. They extended to their students the same invitation their learning community extended to them, to become knowledge makers in a community of knowledge makers. Surely their work points to visions of schooling and expectations for the teaching profession worthy of creating, worthy of keeping.

REFERENCES

Gray, J. (2000). *Teachers at the center: A memoir of the early years of the National Writing Project*. Berkeley, CA: National Writing Project.

Lieberman, A., & Wood, D. (2002). *Inside the National Writing Project: Connecting network learning and classroom teaching*. New York: Teachers College Press.

CHAPTER 1

Overview: Classroom Literacies and Public Culture

Sarah Robbins

This is a book about social literacy in classrooms and its potential contributions to community life. By reporting on the experiences of teachers and students involved in a multiyear curriculum development project—Keeping and Creating American Communities—the authors seek to promote a view of learning as reaching outside the classroom walls both in the content of what is studied and in its influence on society.

These days, much of the conversation about school literacy casts it only as an object of standardized assessment—something to be scrutinized and remediated rather than a positive force in the lives of students and the larger community. At best, current efforts to monitor and manage school literacy aim at ensuring equitable progress among all learners. At worst, this view reduces the complicated social practices of reading, writing, and oral language in classrooms to a newspaper "box score," making test results and attendance rates "public" as a way of designating "failing" schools. The authors of this book see literacy in public education sites as more than a set of test scores. They believe that viewing school literacy as "public" can also mean tapping into its potential for culture-making. Expanding our view of school literacy in this way activates a sense of commitment among teachers and students: Instead of merely being objects of others' analysis, students become empowered agents using literacy to make meaningful contributions to the places where they live—even, ultimately, to the nation's vision of education as a public trust.

This view shifts the meaning of the "public" in "public education" from what has become its everyday meaning back to a stance more in line with the etymology of the word. Indeed, while the *Merriam-Webster's Collegiate Dictionary* (2004) states that the most common meaning of "public" today is "exposed to general view" (a definition consistent with "public" education as constantly being monitored and assessed), it also tells us that the word "public" comes from the Latin *populus* (people), and also means "of, relating to, or affecting all the people or the whole area of a nation or state"; "of, relating to, or being in the service of the community or nation"; "of or relating to business or community interests as opposed to private affairs"; "devoted to the general or national welfare"; and "accessible to or shared by all members of the community." The Keeping and Creating American Communities project has developed a conception of classroom literacy as public work, in line with *all* the definitions of "public" outlined above, not just the first or everyday one.

What kinds of cultural work can students do, once they come to see school literacy as "public" in community-building ways? Here are three snapshots from the K-through-university classrooms where this book's authors teach.

In a rural community in north Georgia, high school students are working in inquiry teams. Partly because their project has already been honored in a local newspaper, they know there will be a public audience eager to read about their research, so they take special care with their writing. Some of the questions they investigate grow out of their teacher's participation in her own research team—when she studied texts about rural life in early twentieth-century Georgia. Doing that inquiry, the teacher became a student again, analyzing memoirs, government documents, historical fiction, public history sites, and photographs of Georgia farming scenes. The teacher then invited her students to become primary researchers and reporters as her own inquiry team had done. The students then combed their local library and historical society, collected oral histories from longtime residents, and scoured old yearbooks at their own school—all part of a project to assemble a school archive.

In downtown Atlanta, an elementary teacher leads her students through the process she used to research a pivotal historical period at her nearby alma mater, Spelman College. She displays Xerox copies of nineteenth-century issues of the alumnae publication, the *Spelman Messenger*. Describing her own efforts to track down leads for an oral history about early Spelman students' leadership in the Black community, she shares her notes from one especially fruitful interview. She and her third graders discuss how the history that her own research team has been assembling will include both "artifacts" from primary-source documents and "personal stories" based on the interviews. Her students' excited reaction to her account leads to a comparable plan: Each of the class members will create an exhibit out of family artifacts and oral histories. By displaying their work in the school hallway, they will introduce themselves to parents visiting for PTA meetings and to students from other classes—publicly building community in their school.

Near a shopping mall in Cobb County, Georgia, a college student enrolled in an interdisciplinary seminar perches on a hillside overlooking a construction site. Where a thick cluster of trees had stood previously, bulldozers churn up red clay. Beside the same busy avenue, a regional shopping mall sprawls. After taking pictures with a digital camera, the student jots down plans for juxtaposing photos with reflections by long-time residents who support or oppose the construction, arguments by scholars studying suburbia, and thoughts from newcomers. She records details carefully, because she knows she will be presenting her research to students from other university classes and, later, posting her PowerPoint to a Web site.

This collection of essays brings together shared principles and reflective learning stories from classrooms like those described above, led by teachers involved in Keeping and Creating American Communities (KCAC). KCAC, an initiative supported by the National Endowment for the Humanities (NEH) and the National Writing Project (NWP), has drawn on scholarship in the humanities and on teachers' own classroom practices to generate an interdisciplinary, writing-intensive curriculum centered in American community life. KCAC teachers and their students have become committed to inquiry research and public writing about where they live.

The KCAC program emphasizes two basic tenets. "Keeping" community invites students to participate in cultural stewardship. In this role students critically examine cultural forces operating in their communities and self-consciously join in civic preservation. Through the "keeping" dimension of KCAC, students do community-based research such as gathering local stories, interpreting public history sites, and analyzing visual culture in their own environments. The "creating" component of the project is equally important, because it encourages students to see themselves as active composers of their communities' identities. As students assemble, analyze, and disseminate their newfound knowledge to public audiences, a clear sense of communal identity emerges.

We developed KCAC's guiding principles partly through participants' conversations in the early stages of our project ("Guiding Principles," 2000–2001). Those principles emphasize the role writing can play in creating communities; the power of collaboration; the potential inherent in cross-level, interdisciplinary study of community life; and the need to view research as open-ended inquiry using a wide range of methods to study diverse cultural artifacts. Other important principles behind our work include a view of communities as continually redefining themselves; an understanding that local communities interact with larger social networks that can be regional, national, and international in scope; an appreciation of social activities and production of material culture as contributing to community formation; and a commitment to proactive citizenship.

One impetus behind our work has come from calls for Americans to revitalize community life. In that vein, KCAC involves students directly in civic culture today to promote their active citizenship in the future. Countering the decline in "civic vitality" and "social capital" that Robert Putnam (2000) has chronicled in *Bowling Alone* (pp. 15, 18–19), KCAC students and teachers build communities in the classroom and beyond. In many diverse settings, they enact a brand of school literacy as proactively public—social in content, method, and aims.

SCHOOL LITERACY AS A SOCIAL ENTERPRISE

For more than a decade, scholarship in literacy studies has urged educators to move beyond viewing literacy as "an isolated skill" to seeing it "as a social process in the daily landscape." Along those lines, in *The New Literacy*, John Willinsky (1990) called for seeing "literacy as actively making something of the world," so that students themselves become "sources of experience and meaning" (pp. 6–7). Such programs move from a view of literacy "as an ability" to literacy as "a purposeful activity" in a social context (p. 9). One dimension much of this work has shared—and a central component of the KCAC model—is a shift from viewing literacy simply as decoding print text to including, and even foregrounding, writing.

As Willinsky (1990) himself admitted, visions of a "new literacy" were not, even in the early 1990s, really new. For one thing, he pointed out, theories for making school literacy "a social process" with an activist agenda have drawn in important ways on the work of John Dewey (p. 4). For another, this agenda has been consistent with what Willinsky described as a "host of different experiments in the teaching of reading and writing," including the Writing Across the Curriculum (WAC) movement, the Bay Area Writing Project, and what he termed "the London School," led by James Britton (pp. 5, 40). Similarly, in their more recent advocacy of inquiry-based learning, Timothy Shannon and Patrick Shannon (2001) have grounded this mission in a heritage going back to Dewey's Chicago Lab School, but also to curricular experiments in the 1920s and 1930s and to "critical pedagogies" from the 1980s and 1990s (pp. 128–132, 134–136).

However familiar calls for organizing classroom instruction around a social view of literacy have become, attempts to enact this vision have sometimes encountered difficulties. In day-to-day instructional practices, Willinsky (1990) suggests, such efforts have bumped up against a lingering tendency to see literacy in individual, cognitive terms and hence the compulsion to emphasize specific students' progress with particular skills. Thus, he argues, even innovative workshop-based programs such as Donald Graves's and Nancie Atwell's run the risk of overemphasizing expressive writing and personal development over the social. Referencing Atwell's work specifically, and despite noting "her students' awakening interest in social issues [such as] peace and pollution," Willinsky characterized many literacy workshop programs as still lacking in commitment to "writing as a critical social enterprise" (p. 55).

But shifting from a cognitive, individual conception of literacy to a genuinely social one is no simple move, Beth Daniell (1999) has shown, especially when the stance cultivated among students *is* critical. For example, Daniell reports on some of the difficulties teacher-scholars influenced by the work of Paolo Freire have encountered when trying to cultivate a "critical consciousness" among their students. One problem, she suggests, has to do with important differences between the culture surrounding the South American peasants with whom Freire did his initial work and that of North American students today. While Daniell acknowledges the appeal—and even the applicability, in some cases—of the idea that students are oppressed people in need of a "critical consciousness," she also reminds us that, in the public classrooms of the United States, "our job is not now, if it ever was, to recruit for a leftist revolution" (p. 401).

Finding productive, ethical teaching practices that promote civic participation without directing students to particular political positions is one of the needs educators must address in our new century. If social literacy is to live at the center of American classroom life, it must recognize multiple viewpoints and life experiences, even while encouraging students to seek shared goals for community action. Then, school literacy will become public in a powerful way—in the content of the curriculum, as we study community culture; in the open, respectful environment we develop for the public space of classroom learning; and in public schools' direct engagement with the world beyond its walls.

KCAC PROJECT HISTORY AND GUIDING PRINCIPLES

The goal of making school literacy public, as outlined above, guided the KCAC program from its first summer institute for teachers in 2000. We named our initiative "Keeping and Creating American Communities" in part to designate the interdisciplinary subject matter of our study (ways that American communities preserve and continually re-form themselves) and the commitment we were making to share what we learned with multiple audiences. We planned to explore American communities with our students as coinvestigators—moving to "take the community as the curriculum" (Shannon & Shannon, 2001, p. 137). We would open up the school to study the places where we live and invite "outside" community members to join us in a variety of ways—collaborating for community-building.

Teachers involved in the KCAC initiative are continuing to implement its principles and practices by building on a sequence of grant-funded activities that included several summer institutes and academic-year continuity programs for more than two dozen educators. The time line of activities that we originally planned for KCAC moved from teachers' working in their own small-group research teams formed around community-oriented themes to having those groups reorganize (or "jigsaw") themselves into different teams using a range of venues to disseminate learning from the project. (See figure 1.1).

In actual practice, the program was extended far beyond the original time line. We progressed through three loose stages of collaboration that overlapped considerably. That is, we focused in the first year on teachers' trying out inquiry-based research into community life themselves, in the second on developing classroom teaching strategies based on those experiences, and in the third on dissemination. But we really began disseminating very early on, as teachers informally shared their experiences with colleagues and students in the first year. Conversely, in what was formally the dissemination stage (with teams focused on workshops, print publications, performances, and Web site venues), we were still doing more community-based research ourselves and with our students. Furthermore, our thematic inquiry practices, curricular experiments, and dissemination efforts—all three phases of project work—have extended beyond the original time line of the program's funding. Nonetheless, a sketch of each stage in our work could be helpful to others.

We concentrated in the first year on trying out interdisciplinary approaches for researching communities, being careful to focus on particular historical eras and spaces. To uncover ways that the places where we live *become* communities, we examined case studies of local cultures constructing themselves as "American" through an array of social texts—including literature, language, cultural events, architecture, public policies, and the physical landscape (Anderson, 1991). In doing so, we drew on Michael Kammen's (1993) proposal that "looking at subnational units of social organization" can promote rich understandings of what it mean "to be an American" (pp. 3, 32–33).

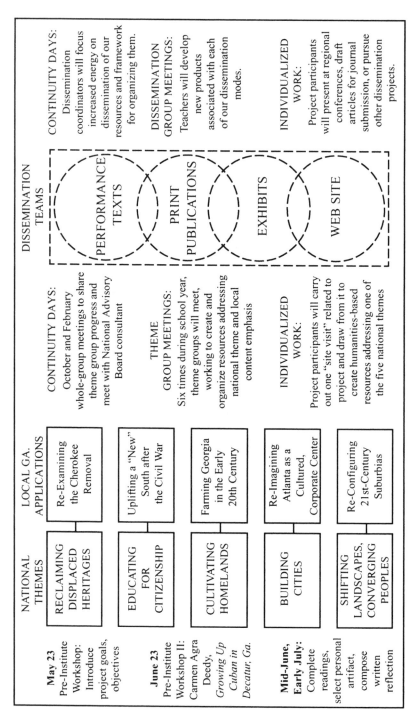

Figure 1.1. Timeline of major activities for the first two years of the Keeping and Creating American Communities program.

We chose five themes to guide our study during that first year: Educating for Citizenship; Reclaiming Displaced Heritages; Building Cities; Cultivating Homelands; and Shifting Landscapes, Converging Peoples. We selected specific examples of each theme to unpack, using Michael Frisch's (2001) analytical model to identify "various components" in each case (p. 197). For instance, for the Reclaiming Displaced Heritages theme, we first chose the specific case of the Cherokee Removal and analyzed forces—political, social, economic, racial, and class based—behind that particular event. For the Building Cities theme, we studied downtown Atlanta in the 1970s–1990s, when the city was recasting itself from a regional town into an international destination with a strong corporate and cultural identity. In that case, our initial explorations ranged from a walking tour of the city to a review of its major economic, cultural, and political developments during the period. Altogether, we spent most of the first summer institute on preliminary investigation of all the themes through site visits, archival research, oral histories, interviews with experts, and discussion of primary texts from multiple disciplines. Then we divided into smaller study teams, with each group researching one theme in depth throughout the first school year.

In year 2 of the program, we concentrated on sharing the results of our initial research *within* our project community and on classroom applications. First, in summer 2001, each team of teacher-researchers facilitated a half-day workshop showcasing both what its members had learned and the interdisciplinary inquiry methods they had used. Second, we prepared to transfer that learning into teaching approaches. Trusting in the NWP's core belief that working as writers enables teachers to do a better job with writing instruction, we expected that doing primary research on community life would be great preparation for inviting our students to do the same. Our trust was rewarded in the classroom, when our students joined KCAC's explorations of American community life.

Since then, teams of students have been collaboratively investigating communal spaces and activities ranging from public history sites to today's subcommunities in Waffle Houses, from rock-climbing parks to subdivision cul-de-sacs and city council meetings. Along the way, they have gathered a wide variety of cultural artifacts—old newspapers; immigrants' coming-to-America stories; maps of neighborhoods before and after major building projects. They have used writing as a powerful, transformative tool to turn those artifacts into exhibits, public performances, printed publications, and multimedia records of community life. They have researched the social practices of small-town churches, inner-city department stores, and suburban banks. They have recovered stories of family life and assembled "maps" of images-with-stories showing the rich cultural diversity in area neighborhoods.

In all these cases, students and their teachers have positioned their study of local communities within a larger cultural context. For instance, they critiqued the competing visions of "America" embedded in a suburban city council's conflict with shop owners setting up Spanish-language signs. Similarly, they researched competing issues of ownership in Atlanta newspaper accounts of a Cherokee tribesman's moving "back" to reclaim land marked off long ago as a state park. These students made connections between shifting American cultural formations and daily community life. Then they shared these interpretations with a range of public audiences.

This book comes out of the final stages of the KCAC project. Having reflected on our learning, we are ready to share our model with other colleagues. It is important to remember, though, as we have tried to show in our stories, that KCAC's initial work was very messy and exploratory, that it was authentic inquiry without a prescribed road map, and that we learned as much from our failures as from our successes. We are still learning—with our students and other members of our growing professional community.

AMERICAN STUDIES AND SOCIAL VIEWS OF COMPOSITION

Part of what kept us going during the challenging early phases of our project was having a collaborative team. Another crucial ingredient was drawing on American Studies approaches to research communities and on recent scholarship in composition to guide ongoing dissemination. Supported by a generous advisory board of leading scholars and teachers from both fields, we eventually developed a far more detailed framework for interdisciplinary inquiry into community culture than the vague but inspiring goals with which we began.

From recent scholarship in American Studies, we took our central inquiry goals. Spurred on by advisory board member Paul Lauter, we repeatedly asked an overarching question about the places where we live: "Why this way, in this time, in this place?" We learned that studying community formation necessarily involves far more than celebration of a discrete local heritage, that we needed to critique the "cultural work" going on in any of the social spaces we explored. We learned to examine the ways that diverse local texts "help[ed] construct the frameworks, fashion the metaphors, create the very language by which people comprehend their experiences and think about their world" (Lauter, 2001, p. 11). Since, as Janice Radway (1999) has observed, "the local and the global" are "intricately intertwined," we aimed for studies of community culture with "a relational and comparative perspective" (p. 24). Overall, the KCAC program has encouraged students and teachers to uncover and critique the forces that have shaped their own local cultures, as subcultures in national and international contexts.

By integrating our American Studies–based inquiry model with related ideas about communities from composition studies, we have placed writing at the center of our curricular framework. Like Bruce McComiskey (2000), we have affiliated ourselves with "social-process rhetorical inquiry," which has "extended the writing process into the world," moving our students' writing "outward (i.e., out of the individual writers' consciousness) toward institutional processes of socialization" (p. 62). Along with McComiskey, we have viewed students' (and our own) writing as "both a way of knowing and acting, a way of understanding the world and also changing it" (p. 62). Thus, although we have placed analysis of cultural practices at the heart of our teaching, we have eschewed the pitfall McComiskey decries in many writing programs: "foreground[ing] cultural politics as material to be mastered" (p. 2). Instead, we have invited students to move from their own examination of culture to writing that composes new communities. In doing so, we have affirmed Jeffrey Grabill's (2001) call to identify social "spaces for change" in communities (pp. xi, 4). At the same time, we consistently remind ourselves of Grabill's warning that community building can lead to "boundaries" being set, with all "the inclusions and exclusions they entail" (p. 90).

We want the boundaries of our professional community to be ever expanding, to include any teachers and students who wish to join our work. In this and other outreach efforts, we affirm one of the core values of the NWP—a commitment to open access and diversity in education. Also influenced by the NWP, of course, is our view of teachers and students as composers (rather than mere consumers) of American communities, and our belief in the centrality of writing as a process for knowing and shaping the world. More specifically, our KCAC work has benefited from a number of our project participants' having been involved in compatible initiatives sponsored by the NWP (NWP Programs, 1995–2003). Through Project Outreach, we learned to place issues of equity and access to learning in the forefront of teaching; and from the NWP's Social Action initiative, our faith in students' ability to shape community life was affirmed. Through the Making American Literatures program, we learned to think of school curricula as changing and changeable (Gere & Shaheen, 2001).

Our work has also been influenced by educational initiatives aimed at "writing for the community," such as those described by Benson, Christian, Goswami, and Gooch (2002), who integrated emphases on "literacy, action research, and 'real-world' writing and publishing" (p. 2). In particular, we are led by the work of Jay Robinson, especially his concept of literacy as "constitutive"—potentially making democratic "habitable spaces" shaped by the agency of purposeful learners (Fleischer & Schaafsma, 1998, pp. xx–xxi). From Robinson and his colleagues, we have found role model programs, such as the Write for Your Life initiative, which invited students to pursue inquiry grounded in "the images and experiences they bring . . . from their home communities" (Stock & Swenson, 1997, p. 154; Robbins, Miesiezek, & Andrews, 2002). We have learned, too, from the Nebraska Writing Project's Rural Voices program, which envisions education aimed at "how to live well, actively, and fully in a given place" (Brooke, 2003, p. ix).

USING STORIES TO PRESENT OUR TEACHING FRAMEWORK

Through this book about classroom successes and challenges, we hope to encourage other educators—in diverse subject areas, instructional levels, and settings—to become community researchers themselves, teachers of community studies, and supporters of students' civic engagement. We have chosen to use the "teacher story" genre because this type of writing honors both the situation-specific workings of the KCAC model in action and the contingent quality of the knowledge that is evolving from our collaboration.

The conceptual framework for community studies outlined above grew out of shared reflection on teaching experiences in diverse contexts. Consistent with Donald A. Schön's (1991) research on reflective practice, our principles for teaching about American communities have been shaped by day-to-day classroom work, even as those practices were being refined by the study we were doing as a professional development community. As scholarship on teacher knowledge-building has shown, educators' understandings of their own teaching tends to be highly contextualized (Stock, 1993). Furthermore, that knowledge (like teacher decision-making) is highly contingent, being constantly guided in new directions by particular student populations and material conditions, such as having different kinds of course schedules or preparing students for standardized tests. Therefore, if all the members of our original KCAC project community were asked to produce a visual diagram of our curricular framework, each of them would probably submit a slightly different picture, even though we certainly all share strong core beliefs and use similar teaching practices. With that variability in mind, telling individual classroom stories provides one of the best ways for us to present our framework: We hope that the diverse implementation approaches recorded here will make it clear that KCAC's vision for community studies can be tailored to any setting, that our model is flexible and organic rather than prescriptive. At the same time, however, readers will find many connections and points of agreement. For example, a number of us address questions about how to integrate community studies into the classroom while also maintaining a focus on district, university, state, and national standards for disciplinary instruction.

One thing all our essays have in common is their emphasis on reflection and on storytelling's role in reflection. We hope that they can serve as models for teacher knowledge-making through narrative writing. As Mary Jalongo and her colleagues (Jalongo, Isenbert, & Gerbracht, 1995) have found, "Personal narratives are an effective way for educators to arrange, understand, and organize their experiences, giving them a shape, a theme, a frame" (p. 31).

One of our goals in writing this book together has been to make *our* literacy practices public, to show our model for professional growth in action. The teacher knowledge represented in this collection synthesizes a two-step process through reports on what the authors learned by doing community studies themselves and how they adapted their learning to reform their teaching. Thus, our essays provide both classroom-tested approaches for using a flexible curricular model and a unique record of one teaching community's professional growth.

ORGANIZATION OF THE BOOK

Part I, Community Studies in the Classroom (Chapters 2–7), focuses on making communities' cultural work a topic for school study and on fostering a strong sense of community among our students. Here, we offer practical ideas for curriculum development and reflective analyses of this approach as a "public" kind of teaching. In linking teachers' new instructional strategies with their own learning experiences on KCAC inquiry teams, the essays in this section often underscore connections between teacher professional growth and classroom reform.

Along those lines, Sylvia Martinez stresses the personal dimension inherent in community studies in Chapter 2, "Discovering the Power of My Place." Sylvia first recounts her own journey, including doing research on suburban life with teacher colleagues on her KCAC inquiry team, and, later, reexamining her hometown of San Antonio, Texas, through a photographic lens. The second part of Sylvia's story demonstrates how she applied her learning to guide her students' personal discoveries based on photography and writing.

Whereas Sylvia teaches in an urbanizing neighborhood, Linda Templeton works in a community changing from rural to suburban. As Templeton explains in Chapter 3, "From Personal Research to Community Learning," she invited all the students in her high school English classes—newcomers and longtime residents alike—to research the rural heritage of Paulding County, Georgia. By assembling their projects into a classroom museum, Templeton's students combined an affirmation of growing diversity in their community with an honoring of its past heritage.

Both Martinez and Templeton approach community studies with a similar aim: nurturing a culture of acceptance in the classroom. Chapter 4, "A City Too Busy to Reflect?" may seem to be headed in the opposite direction, as LeeAnn Lands spurs her students to confront cultural conflict. Actually, Lands also seeks to build community. But her different instructional context—teaching public history in a university setting—leads to a different method: constructive debate about public exhibits grounded in controversial topics.

Like Lands, Patsy Hamby (Chapter 5) turned to history to explore community studies. After researching the Cherokee Removal during the first phase of KCAC's program, Hamby chose one novel, Robert Conley's *Mountain Windsong* (1992), to teach. By combining collaborative learning activities with opportunities for students to share artifacts from their personal lives, Hamby and her students created their own classroom community while weaving together the three strands from Conley's narrative.

Shifting from history to cultural geography, Leslie Walker in "I Belong to This Place" (Chapter 6) organizes KCAC curricular innovation around a spatial metaphor. Walker takes the reader along, as an excursion to sites within walking distance of her high school becomes a research experience. Students learn new ways of "reading" the environment through observation enhanced by reflective writing.

In "Composing Communities" (Chapter 7) Linda Stewart also emphasizes place-based inquiry. Stewart shows how inviting students to do primary research on the spaces where they live has re-formed her classroom as well. Stewart's students now ask important questions of every space they encounter (e.g., "What isn't there?" and "Why not?"), then seek to "uncover the voices of our culture that have been ignored or suppressed."

In Part II, Public Literacy Projects and Civic Culture (Chapters 8–12), we highlight applications of our model that planned from the start to engage with communities beyond the classroom through collaboration and public dissemination. Said another way, whereas Chapters 2–7 emphasize the "keeping" element of KCAC, Chapters 8–12 draw primarily on the "creating" component, accenting ways in which students have moved outside the classroom to become culture-making agents. These authors present themselves and their students as public intellectuals, true stewards of community culture.

In "Learning to Write as a Community" (Chapter 8), Traci Blanchard describes how her new way of fulfilling her district's research paper requirement drew on her own experiences as webmaster for KCAC, when she learned how to support collaboration and writing for the very public audience of the World Wide Web. Her new model for school research led her students to work in teams, using primary-research techniques to explore topics with significance beyond their classroom, and to develop ways of presenting their findings to public audiences.

In "Writing a Museum" (Chapter 9), Bonnie Webb also concentrates on the power of publication. Webb's story about middle school students' writing on the Martin Luther King Center and historic site points to important long-term implications. As Webb explains, "When students are invited to go beyond 'visiting'" a museum to interpreting it in cultural context, "they begin to move from observation to genuine social consciousness," becoming "future curators of their culture."

In Chapter 10, Mimi Dyer singles out another publication avenue that KCAC teachers found particularly effective: performance. Dyer argues that preparing for a public performance in itself builds community whether her high school students are creating historical skits for their own classroom or a more elaborate drama on the Cherokee Removal for a large audience from an area elementary school.

Scott Smoot, like Dyer, celebrates performance. But Smoot's essay, "Composing History" (Chapter 11), takes more of a case study approach, detailing the start-to-production experience of a particular project that used music to synthesize the material his middle school students gathered from family oral histories. Smoot's story includes details of his own instructional plan, but also evidence of its effect on students, parents, and other audience members.

On an even larger scale, Peggy Corbett's "History Happened Here" (Chapter 12) portrays community studies' impact on the place where she works and lives. Corbett describes team research projects her students carried out to study the rural heritage of Canton, Georgia. As public writing about their research attracted growing attention, Corbett explains, local leaders from the historical society became involved, and other teachers joined in, trying their own versions of community studies. Corbett found herself transformed from a classroom teacher to a district-level teacher mentor, leading other educators into new fields of culture making.

CONTRIBUTIONS FROM STUDENTS AND COLLEAGUES

In every chapter of this book, we record stories from the daily life of class-rooms. We have identified our schools and university sites by name, hoping through that choice, and with demographic details about each student population, to convey a clear sense of the actual public places where we work. Certainly, with these locations as our primary sites of observation and analysis, students have been major shapers of our knowledge. We are grateful to all our students for having contributed so substantially to this project. To safeguard their privacy, we use pseudonyms throughout the book when referring to individual students, except in cases where they have requested to be identified by name. In cases where we quote from student writing, we have secured written permission from the authors and (if they are under 18 years of age) from a parent. Here, as in all other writing decisions made for this book, our aim has been to recognize the potentially powerful ways that classroom learning can become a part of public culture.

NOTE

For further details of the projects described in this volume and the themes they addressed, the reader is referred to the KCAC Web site at: http://kcac.kennesaw/ edu/

REFERENCES

Anderson, B. (1991). *Imagined communities: Reflections on the origin and spread of nationalism*. Urbana: University of Illinois Press.

Benson, C., Christian, S., Goswami, D., & Gooch, W. H. (2002). *Writing to make a difference: Classroom projects for community change*. New York: Teachers College Press.

Brooke, R. (Ed.). (2003). *Rural voices: Place-conscious education and the teaching of writing*. New York: Teachers College Press, 2003.

Conley, R. (1992). *Mountain windsong*. Norman: University of Oklahoma Press.

Daniell, B. (1999). Narratives of literacy: Connecting composition to culture. *CCC: College Composition and Communication, 50*, 393–410.

Fleischer, C., & Schaafsma, D. (Eds.). (1998). *Literacy and democracy: Teacher research and composition studies in pursuit of habitable spaces*. Urbana: National Council of Teachers of English.

Frisch, M. (2001). Prismatics, multivalence, and other riffs on the millennial moment: Presidential address to the American Studies Association, 13 October 2000. *American Quarterly, 53*, 193–231.

Gere, A. R., & Shaheen, P. (Eds.). (2001). *Making American literatures*. Urbana: National Council of Teachers of English.

Grabill, J. T. (2001). *Community literacy programs and the politics of change*. Albany: State University of New York Press.

Guiding principles. (2000–2001). In *Keeping and creating American communities*. Retrieved February 29, 2004, from http://kcac.kennesaw.edu/curricular_program/guiding_principles/gprinc.html

Jalongo, M. R., Isenbert, J. P., & Gerbracht, G. (1995). *Teachers' stories: From personal narrative to professional insight*. San Francisco: Jossey-Bass.

Kammen, M. (1993). The problem of American exceptionalism: A reconsideration. *American Quarterly, 45*, 1–43.

Lauter, P. (2001). *From Walden Pond to Jurassic Park: Activism, culture, and American studies*. Durham: Duke University Press.

McComiskey, B. (2000). *Teaching composition as a social process*. Logan: Utah State University Press.

Merriam-Webster's collegiate dictionary (11th ed.). (2004). Retrieved February 29, 2004, from http://www.merriam-webstercollegiate.com/cgi-bin/collegiate?va=public&x=35&y=5

NWP Programs. (1905–2003). In *National Writing Project*. Retrieved February 29, 2004, from http://www.writingproject.org/Programs/projects.html

Putnam, R. (2000). *Bowling alone: The collapse and revival of American community*. New York: Simon & Schuster.

Radway, J. (1999). "What's in a name?" Presidential address to the American Studies Association, November 20, 1998. *American Quarterly, 51*, 1–32.

Robbins, S., Miesiezek, M., & Andrews, B. (2002). Promoting a relevant classroom literacy. In R. P. Yagelski & S. A. Leonard (Eds.), *The relevance of English: Teaching that matters in students' lives* (pp. 157–182). Urbana: National Council of Teachers of English.

Schön, D. A. (Ed.). (1991). *The reflective turn: Case studies in and on educational practice*. New York: Teachers College Press.

Shannon, T., & Shannon, P. (2001). Classrooms in the community: From curriculum to pedagogy. In S. Boran & B. Comber (Eds.), *Critiquing whole language and classroom inquiry* (pp. 123–141). Urbana: National Council of Teachers of English.

Stock, P. L. (1993). The function of anecdote in teacher research. *English Education, 25*, 173–187.

Stock, P. L. & Swenson, J. (1997). The Write for Your Life project: Learning to serve by serving to learn. In L. Adler-Kassner, R. Crooks, & A. Watters (Eds.), *Writing the community: Concepts and models for service-learning in composition* (pp. 153–166). Washington, DC: American Association of Higher Education.

Willinsky, J. (1990). *The new literacy: Redefining reading and writing in the schools.* New York: Routledge.

PART I

Community Studies
in the Classroom

Students, teachers, and the classroom space change when the curriculum takes on a community studies focus. In this section of our book we invite you to see such change in action. Each of the authors describes a teacher's experience inviting students to research local culture and explains the impact that this process has had on the classroom community itself.

Reading the narratives in this section as a group, you will see some recurring themes. Students and teachers begin to think more critically about the relationship between individuals and the larger community, and they try out new ways to represent their personal place there. The classroom itself becomes a space for refining citizenship skills, including productive strategies for dealing with controversy. Along the way, the curriculum grows, becoming bigger than the classroom. Diversity becomes more than an abstract topic, as learners' unique, individual cultures become subjects for shared interpretation. At the same time, when students move "outside" the boundaries of the school or university to research where they live, the values they identify as crucial in those public settings are brought back "inside" to shape the construction of classroom knowledge and culture.

While we hope you will draw upon this section's narratives to try community-oriented teaching approaches in your own classroom, we also encourage you to note the important "backstories" behind the curricular innovations outlined here. As some authors describe specifically and others reference more indirectly, each of these teacher-writers tried out strategies for researching local culture herself before inviting her students to do so. Thus, the authors reflect upon multiple dimensions of professional development: their own experiences studying community, their efforts to engage students in similar research, and the effects those instructional practices had on classroom life.

CHAPTER 2

Discovering the Power of My Place: Personal Journeys to a Community Focus

Sylvia Martinez

"Say *cheese*, Ms. Martinez!" As a smile began to form on my face, my eyes blinked from the bright flash of a disposable camera. "I am working on my project!" Stephen exclaimed. My smile fully developed at that point as I realized that one of my general education tenth-grade students had not only taken ownership of our class project, but he was relishing his ownership. This was unusual for students at Campbell High School.

My school is 35% White, 43% Black, 14% Hispanic, 5% Asian, and 2% multiracial. We also have 21 other races and ethnicities represented. Our diversity is not only racial but also economic, as I have students who live in large houses in swim/tennis communities and those who live in small, rundown apartments or subsidized housing. The differences in race, class, and ethnicity, however, are not our main focus, probably because we are so diverse. Students are very accepting and welcoming of one another, and while they recognize the differences, they don't want them to be divisive.

Another bond that students share is that many are not natives to the local community. Because they have not lived long in Smyrna, many of them do not consider themselves to be a part of the area, so I wanted them to realize that they are still a part of our community and that their sense of place is not solely based on where they reside.

The days following this initial encounter were filled with joys, triumphs, frustrations, and ultimately successes as I ventured with my class on the journey to discover the power of place. For the project, students used photography with reflection and analysis as they recorded important places in their lives. We were not only conducting authentic primary research, but we were personalizing community studies to discover how people and places interact together. This journey drew my students into their research. They were not reading about people, places, and events completely unrelated to them; instead, they were exploring their *own* people, places, and events. They took ownership of the research, making it personal and therefore more relevant to their lives. This is their story as much as it is mine.

EMBARKING ON THE JOURNEY

But I must back up to the beginning, for the germ of Stephen's exclamation actually began a year earlier. Through the Keeping and Creating American Communities (KCAC) project, I had been reading about and researching community, which led me to unravel the role of community in our local and national world. A recurring term in our readings, discussions, and excursions was *place*. Honestly, when I first began to think of place and what it meant, it was merely a word to represent buildings and specific locations. I thought that there was no sense in exploring such a boring word that would surely be marked down as poor use of diction! But, after reading *The Power of Place* by Dolores Hayden (1999), *Seedfolks* by Paul Fleischman (1999), and *Crabgrass Frontier* by Kenneth T. Jackson (1985), my mind was filled with many exciting and provoking thoughts. I realized that the discussion of place was not only widespread, but also intriguing. I began to understand that community creates a sense of place synonymous with belonging, and in order to create a community where people belong, one must find a place where people *can* belong. That place becomes the community.

Hayden (1999) states that "an individual's sense of place is both a biological response to the surrounding physical environment and a cultural creation" (p. 16). This observation sparked the idea that place included not only the physical space, but more important, the person. This notion was further explained, or should I say complicated, by Jackson's (1985) comment regarding the role of the front porch in the "pre-suburban" United States: "The front porch was the physical expression of neighborliness and community" (p. 280). Thinking about how the front porch represents community, I quickly realized that it is the people who make the place, not the place itself. This image of people interacting in a shared space began to solidify my assertion that community is powerful, and the source of its power is its people.

Reading the short young-adult novella *Seedfolks* (Flesichman, 1999) strengthened this thinking. The engaging and widely accessible book combined the physical representation with the human representation of community. In this story of neighbors rallying together through the planting of a garden, a community is created in a physical place where people interact. The place created would not be what it was without both the people and the space. Thus this author, too, explores the idea that a sense of community is rooted in a sense of place.

Working with the KCAC project, I was able to read and experiment and then return to my thinking process a number of times. Knowing that recursive learning is crucial, I realized it was OK to give myself the time necessary to properly understand what I was embarking on. Once I felt I had a handle on what others felt about the power of place and community, I knew I wanted to share this concept with my students. But at the same time, I was drawn to defining my personal space. I knew that in order to share with my students this powerful concept of community and place being intertwined, I must first explore and experience it myself.

Within the KCAC project, the larger group was divided into five strands exploring how communities are formed. My group's thematic area of research was Shifting Landscapes, Converging Peoples, which centered on suburban life and culture. Our research was cumulative, occurring during the first summer and into the first school year of the project. We researched suburbia in our local area in order to discover how specific communities, such as subdivisions and shopping centers, were reconciling their histories with the new immigrant cultures.

One area of interest was Smyrna, where Campbell High School was built. The first time my team of teacher researchers and I ventured out, we were unsure of the path to take. We started by simply driving around the most commonly viewed areas, such as the newly developed community center, library, police station, and city hall. In the process, we noticed there were many new town homes and restaurants also being built, so we took photographs with a digital camera and picked up some literature geared for newcomers.

As we flipped through one guide, a few pages jumped out at us. Most obvious was an advertisement written in Spanish for people to be counted for current census numbers. I was struck by this ad and the idea that a whole other culture of the Smyrna community existed and that we had to explore it. We drove less than a mile around the corner to find an old shopping strip mall filled with Spanish-speaking businesses. As we photographed this area, I began to wonder how the patrons of this enclave combined to create a community with the sponsors of the aesthetically pleasing new community center area.

After this initial trip, we began to examine the pictures and think about what they communicated about Smyrna. As I studied the photos, the idea of people creating the community became evident. Many people utilize the community center of Smyrna, and at the same time, many people visit the strip mall of Spanish-speaking stores. This activity helped me learn the value of photography and how powerful it can be in capturing the essence of a thought or an emotion; still, I was only researching someone else's history and community. I needed to discover my own place, and the best place to begin was with my hometown and with my family, in San Antonio, Texas.

PERSONALIZING THE JOURNEY

The power of place fresh in my mind, in December 2001, I returned to San Antonio, a large city rich in culture and heritage, for my family's traditional Christmas celebration. Of mixed race (Mexican/Spanish/Irish), I never really claimed one ethnicity as my sole culture. Despite these feelings, I love returning to San Antonio because being surrounded by the faces, voices, colors, and food of my Mexican heritage helps me to feel more connected and embraced by a larger community.

Part of our family tradition is to have dinner with my uncle and aunt on my father's side at our favorite restaurant. This eatery has been around for many years and is located in the predominantly Spanish-speaking neighborhood my father and his immediate family grew up in. We always listen to stories told by my dad, aunt, and uncle about the experiences they had in and near this place. On the way home from dinner one night, I began to ask my father questions about the buildings that he grew up around. I asked where they were and what happened there. For the first time, it seemed I was really interested in knowing where he came from. I realized that *his* place was the beginning of *my* place. It was my heritage.

Then I thought back to what I had begun to learn in Smyrna regarding the value of photographs, so my father, mother, and I returned to the neighborhood the next day with a camera. Dad took me to various buildings, such as the first house he remembers living in, the corner grocery store he frequented, the fire station he used to fight behind, and his elementary school. He told me stories as we went along. I smiled as I took a picture of the grocery store where he recalled stealing candy with his brothers, only to find out years later that the owner knew it and didn't mind the "stealing." As I took a picture of the first house he lived in, I thought how small it was and then felt guilty as he explained how close he felt to his family while they were there.

Probably most poignant was visiting my uncle's house, which is where my father and his brothers and sister spent most of their childhood and where I remember spending time with my "Mama Grande," my grandmother. Neither of us could believe how small the house and yard actually were; both my dad and I remembered its being larger than life. These moments continued as we traveled around the neighborhood and my father recounted more stories and how the places had changed over time. I was a student of my father once again. Not only had this visit cemented the connection between people and places; it illustrated that family and place are also intertwined.

The next day, I went with a childhood friend to rediscover my own personal places. As we visited our old schools, hangouts, and neighborhood play spots, we remembered the people and experiences that made those places significant. As I perused the pictures later, I discovered, just as I had with my father's stories, that there was a common thread between our places despite the generation gap. For both my father and me, the similarity was the people connected to our buildings. The memories that came were filled with faces, emotions, and relationships.

I finally realized how and why those places interacted with people to create my cultural community. Then I knew I had to bring this revelation to my students. I owed it to them to help them begin not only to discover their places, but also to uncover the people and memories that really make up those places. My students are so diverse and have such unique experiences; yet they are not encouraged to share their stories. My personal experience in San Antonio changed my view of community and helped me reconnect to my family and community. I wanted my students to have a similar experience.

PROMOTING THE JOURNEY

I am a passionate teacher; I want my students to be passionate about something in their lives because passion creates a need to know more. If students want to know more, then they will take ownership of their learning and their decision-making. They will become more responsible, active learners if their interest is piqued in the classroom. When one—or better yet, all—of my students discover(s) their passions, then I have achieved one of my major goals. In the community project experience, many of my students discovered that they were passionate about where they come from.

Initially, I envisioned the "My Place" project as students taking pictures of specific places where they experienced meaningful moments.

Through photography and writing, my students would explore the power and significance of their "places." I imagined beautiful, elaborately designed scrapbooks perfectly depicting the stories of their lives. I imagined every project being turned in on time and presented eloquently and dramatically. I imagined students listening attentively with hungry eyes and ears. I imagined students expressing their gratification for my having helped them discover where they truly come from. Now, if you are a passionate teacher, then I know you have imagined similar results. And as is the case in most classrooms, the results were far from what I expected, but they turned out to be exactly what I wanted. I expected a finished product and a concise, yet meaningful, lesson learned about community—the lesson that people and community are undoubtedly connected. What happened in my classroom was far from concise, and the meaningful lesson was much deeper than anything I could conceive.

My original goals were for my students:

- To recognize the places in our lives that hold significance
- To uncover the significant memories in our lives
- To recognize that our stories and places have value
- To use writing as a tool to represent and communicate the individual's definition of place
- To reflect on the discoveries made during the student's exploration of place

When I actually introduced the assignment, I gave purposefully vague instructions. I did not mention the idea of people being a part of place. I had just begun to explore that concept myself and still didn't quite understand it. I wanted to see what my students would come up with. As I finished explaining, I saw blank stares, questioning looks, and a smattering of frowning faces. Apparently I had not given enough details.

"What are we supposed to do?"

"Who's gonna buy the camera?"

"How many pictures?"

"I just moved here. No place here is important to me."

"What do we have to write about?"

Not too effectively, I attempted to hide my frustration, and then tried again to explain my idea. "I want you to take pictures of places that hold significance for you and with each picture write a caption describing the place and its significance."

A few nods and some scribbling sounds followed. I believed I was making progress. The due date was in a few weeks, so I decided to wait and see what came in. Over the next few days I was fielding many individual questions regarding the project, so I decided to explain it once again to the whole class. I orally modeled the thinking process that occurred when I embarked on my picture-taking journey to discover my places in San Antonio, which helped to give my students focus. I found myself giving more specific examples, including the subjects of my own pictures and my father's pictures. The examples were helpful because the objects I photographed illustrated to my students a definition of *significant* as I meant for them to address in the assignment. Things were becoming clearer to them.

Finally, D-Day (Due Date) arrived. I was excited and a bit apprehensive. I asked, "Any volunteers to present their project first?"

"Do I get extra credit for going first?"

"No. Any volunteers? Anybody? Does anyone want to go first?"

"I don't think I did my project right."

"I didn't choose buildings because I didn't grow up here. Am I gonna get points off for not having buildings?"

"I don't think I did mine right either."

The wide variety of responses indicated that there were many questions that needed to be answered. I hoped that as we listened to one another's projects, the answers would become evident. As students presented their projects, I saw pictures and heard stories that described each student's individuality. The "places" they presented were varied. Kyle photographed his poetry journal since he feels he can truly be himself when he is writing in it. Stephen showed a picture of his mother's car because he and his mother spend their only quality time driving to and from places, because of her extensive and time-consuming job. Kerry photographed her favorite chair that she used for everything from reading for school to thinking about her mother, who died a number of years ago.

Frederick displayed a picture of his family's kitchen table, where time is spent eating and talking. He said this is where the family connects those few times a week. Dezrick showed a picture of a dresser drawer that served as a bed for his baby brother. This student also included a picture of his grandmother's gravestone with dirt all around it. His analysis explained the reason for the dirt; it was there because the graves of African Americans in that cemetery were in the untended areas.

Still, after hearing their presentations and reexamining their writing that night, I felt my students weren't quite "there" yet. They had identified places, but their analyses of the pictures indicated that they didn't understand the connection of place, people, and community. Most of their descriptions were simply physical ones without their truly examining how and why these "places" were significant. They had made the first step in discovery, but they had not yet realized exactly what they had done. I was unsure of what direction in which to move at this point, so I had to revisit my own explorations to process what was occurring in my classroom.

Our KCAC group participates in a Listserv where we post thoughts, questions, and ideas. I posted my thoughts about the project, what we did, and what I received from my students. Then I simply asked, in an almost desperate plea, "What do I do now?" We discussed the importance of giving my students time to discover their places, as well as introducing them to a new way of approaching learning. At the encouragement of KCAC colleagues, I decided to have my students revisit all the projects and reflect on the experience of creating them. Often students turn an assignment in, receive a grade, and file the assignment away in a folder or notebook, never to be looked at again. I wanted to demonstrate the value in revisiting their work and using metacognition to think about it as well. I had experienced this type of evaluation and analysis in my own work with the KCAC project and wanted to allow them similar opportunities.

REVISITING THE JOURNEY

About 2 weeks after the photographs first came in, I had students put their desks in a circle. I gave them a sheet with five questions to respond to as we examined each student's project. The task was to pass each project around and jot down notes responding to the prompts.

MY PLACE PROJECT EVALUATION (ORIGINAL VERSION)

1. What kinds of places did you and your classmates choose?
2. What surprised you about what you observed in the projects?
3. What is not there?
4. Pick at least one phrase or sentence that you admire about someone's project.
5. In a paragraph define *place*.

Questions erupted:

"What do you mean by what surprised us?"
"What does 'not there' mean?"
"Do we have to do this to get our grade?"
"What is the point of this?"

By then, I was a bit apprehensive about giving too much guidance, so I was intentionally vague with my responses to their questions. I encouraged them to think beyond the literal question. I told them to think about what things they expected to see pictures of but did not. I tried to guide them to discovering their own answers instead of giving them my own.

Initially, there were mumbles and complaints throughout the room, but the students eventually settled down and began to write. Most of the responses I got were empty of critical thought. Still the comments were more about the actual aesthetic value of the product and less about the cultural context. They did not or could not reflect on the project as a representation of community life, composed of place and people together. They did not understand critiquing a cultural document. Their responses further solidified my realization that my students had discovered their places but they hadn't discovered the significance of their discovery. Yet I was not ready to give up on them; I wanted to push them to try and think of their work in a more critical way. I wanted them to explore the thought processes and decision-making that took place as they created their projects.

The following reflection included four overhead questions or prompts:

1. Describe what you liked about the project and why
2. Describe what you disliked about the project and why
3. What did you learn by completing this project?
4. What did you discover about yourself and your places?

Then I gave them time to work on their responses in class:

"Are we still working on this my place thing?"
"Is this the same grade or a new grade?"
"What if we didn't dislike anything about the project?"
"What if we didn't like anything about the project?"
"Why are we still talking about this project? Wasn't it finished a while ago?"

Despite initial griping, they actually had things to say in these reflections. Their responses were much more personal and thoughtful this time, not necessarily poetic and eloquent in detail, but definitely more reflective. Frederick wrote, "I realized that my places are close to home." Jessica wrote, "I discovered that my places were really helpful to me because I met good friends there." Stephen commented, "I discovered my mother is the biggest part of my life." Tiffany reflected, "I learned how the most unimportant places are important." Colby wrote, "[I appreciated] learning how a place can be so special to you."

They made the connections between the people in their lives and the subjects of the pictures, between community and the places they chose to present. They were able to verbalize that the pictures were more than just pictures—they were symbols of something deeper and more meaningful, such as comfort, security, and safety. They discovered that they had their own unique spaces and that those spaces were valuable not only to them but also to their families, friends, teachers, and fellow students.

ANALYSIS AND IMPLICATIONS

The idea of authentic research was foreign to me at one time; now I understand that my students were conducting authentic research through photography and oral history. This research was real in that they were actively searching for their own communities and creating them. They were not rehashing what someone else had already discovered; rather, they were discovering themselves. The idea of sharing their research with their friends and family was meaningful as they came to understand that these were important discoveries. During the course of the project, students often came to my room and told me that they had shown their friends the project; they were clearly excited to talk about what they were doing. And when they told me about sharing with their parents, their eyes lit up, and I could see the sense of accomplishment on their faces.

Knowing that they wanted to have a wider audience gave me a sense of fulfillment because I knew they were excited about their work. We created our own cultural community in our classroom as I watched students try to understand one another's choice of subject matter. As the semester progressed, my students continually referred to various characters being a part of a community or a community's not accepting someone. My students had come face to face with the people and places that defined who they were. They wanted to apply that newfound understanding to everything they encountered. Their sense of place was not only discovered, but was also enlarged and enhanced through the experience of the My Place project.

At the end of the semester, I always have students reflect on the work and experiences in the class. They are asked to write about a piece of literature or project that was particularly meaningful. Several students chose to write about the My Place project. Their comments capture the impact of the project.

Colby said, "The My Place project gave us a chance to share things and places that are important to us. It also gave us a way to help people understand where we came from and what we are all about." She had grasped the powerful idea that our community is in a sense a birthplace. It helps to create who we are and who we will become. She recognized that in order to understand a person, it is most important to first understand where she or he came from. Additionally, Dezrick observed:

> Growing up where I did there weren't too many ways to go. In order to survive many people did things they weren't proud of which made them hate other people. Which affected me in the way I act today because sometimes I can't stand being around other people. My Place project showed me that people can and need to look out for each other to build a strong community. Hopefully I can start and teach my kids so they can start to build a strong community when they get grown.

Dezrick's reflection is powerful because he has realized that this project taught him more than community understanding; it also taught him civic responsibility. He appreciates that communities help to create who we are and therefore it is our responsibility to keep our communities strong.

This journey that emphasized the extraordinary quality of ordinary places and events was powerful because it not only was personal for me, but it also became personal for my students. They walked away from the experience having grown in a way that I could not have brought about by lecturing or reading to them. I watched as my students became proactive citizens by recovering and reclaiming family ties, critiquing the true meaning of public and private spaces, and creating projects that reflected the dynamic value of their own personal communities.

Most adults have not become this type of active member of the community. An important factor for engaging students in this process of discovery is freedom. Students must be a part of the process. They must first collaborate with one another to create their own community in the classroom before even venturing outside the walls. Once they have built the foundation of community, they are much more likely to explore places and subjects they might never have before. Through this exploration, passions are discovered. I had KCAC colleagues who believed in the power of community and discovery. And because of them, my students took this project—combining photography with reflection and analysis—and made it relevant to their lives. They were unafraid to take the journey to discover their place and in the process became passionate, active learners.

REFERENCES

Fleischam, P. (1999). *Seedfolks.* New York: HarperTrophy.

Hayden, D. (1999). *The power of place: Urban landscapes as public history.* Cambridge, MA: MIT Press.

Jackson, K. T. (1985). *Crabgrass frontier: The suburbanization of the United States.* New York: Oxford University Press.

CHAPTER 3

From Personal Research to Community Learning

Linda Templeton

I bequeath myself to the dirt to grow from the grass I
   love,
If you want me again look for me under your boot-soles.

You will hardly know who I am or what I mean,
But I shall be good health to you nevertheless,
And filter and fibre your blood.

Failing to fetch me at first keep encouraged.
Missing me one place search another,
I stop some where waiting for you.
                              —Walt Whitman, *Song of Myself*

No matter where we live today—in places that are rural, suburban, or urban—the land where our homes exist began simply . . . as land. Community inquiry captures stories and preserves heritage, while revealing the intricacies of a community structure. A valuable result of such an investigation is a greater appreciation of our places in this community structure. Over several years of working with students in my classroom and my Keeping and Creating American Communities (KCAC) colleagues, I have developed a series of activities that blend the rural and suburban cultures within our community, promoting a broader understanding of what it means to belong to a community that is rapidly changing, while celebrating the old, rural heritage of our past. My project design helps teachers, students, parents, and community members face the challenge of increasing diversity by creating opportunities for exploring differences within our classrooms, in the hope that we can then celebrate them to promote a culture of tolerance. The guiding principle of my project involves students researching their changing rural communities. This research leads them to discover local heritages and embrace changing landscapes in communities experiencing transition between rural and suburban life. As the project has evolved over the years, I have added components and enhanced others, establishing a method for creating a knowledgeable classroom, embracing diversity, and learning with students.

DOING MY OWN RESEARCH FIRST

When I first developed this curriculum, I lived and worked in Paulding County, a small rural community located in northwest Georgia. Paulding County does not have a major highway within it or even touching its boundaries, nor does it have an industrial tax base; however, it allows builders to keep expanding neighborhoods, changing farmlands to golf estates. Most of the citizens are either self-employed or drive into Atlanta for their jobs. Commutes are sometimes 50 miles and up to an hour each way along two-lane roads jammed bumper to bumper with cars, trucks, and school buses. The maximum speed many days is 45 mph, if there isn't an accident. The tranquil country setting in Paulding County helps to make the long commute worthwhile, though, and many people have been doing it for years. While the student body increases in diversity with each year, East Paulding's population is relatively stable, with most students remaining at the school for the full 4 years. For instance, during the year described here, I did not lose one student through transferring or dropping out.

Since I am not from Paulding County, I knew that I needed to know more about my community before I could ask my students to do a research project about where they live. One of the first steps I took in establishing community-based inquiry myself led me to visit the Paulding County Historical Museum. Through the KCAC project, I knew that I could become a proactive citizen by studying my community's preservation choices before adding my own and my students' stories as new records of our area. By researching the community before my students, I could lead them to understand the importance in the "keeping" process to shape our own "creating" of new texts that represent the kinds of communities to which we all belong.

The museum—sponsored by the Paulding County Historical Society and housed in an old one-room schoolhouse—displays many artifacts that have been donated by various individuals and families. I saw old school desks—one from the Black High School (real name)—donations of personal family treasures, clothes dating back to the 1800s, and much more. The museum curator, paying special attention to the story of his brother's service in World War II, gave me a personal tour, complete with pictures, letters, and newspaper articles. While the contents of the museum held my interest, I still had unanswered questions about the history of Paulding County. In looking back, I should have asked the curator more probing questions. However, my southern upbringing discouraged me from asking them out loud.

But as I looked at pieces of clothing, I did wonder how those hardworking people could ever complete their chores in button-up shoes, laced-up dresses, and brogans. As I examined the museum's contents, it was the *absence of presence* that I noticed—not the displayed items. The phrase *absence of presence* comes from our KCAC group's visit, during one of our summer institutes, to New Echota, former capital of the Cherokee Nation. As our group walked around the site, we felt that something/someone was missing, so we began using the phrase "absence of presence," from Gerald Vizenor's (1998) study of Native American culture, because we felt that many of the Cherokee views, opinions, and stories were absent.

Now as I stood in the middle of this museum in my hometown, those same feelings of absence returned. *Where were the untold stories of the farmers, the African Americans, the Native Americans?* I asked those questions because when I had examined pamphlets at the museum, I saw that the writers mentioned that it was a farming community, that there were slaves at one time, and that the Creek and Cherokee had been a part of the territory; however, the stories of these groups were missing from the local museum.

During my first year of KCAC participation, I read several books directly associated with early 20th century rural life in Georgia. Those books told some of the missing stories of the poor white farmers, African Americans, and Native Americans in our region. We read and discussed Caroline Miller's (1933) novel *Lamb in His Bosom*, which relates the saga of the struggling people of the Georgia backwoods, who never owned a slave or planned to fight a war. The novel explores the social customs and harsh realities of the Georgia dirt farmer, experienced through the poor existence of one family. Another text we read was Jimmy Carter's (2000) *An Hour Before Daylight*, a nonfiction account of his growing up on a farm in South Georgia in the years between the two world wars. While his family was more comfortable than most, Carter gives the reader insight into the demanding life of a farmer in the first half of the 20th century, revealing the trials and tribulations of the time through his relationships with share-cropping families and their children, who became his best friends. Likewise,

Raymond Andrews's (1990) memoir, *Last Radio Baby*, tells a similar story in south Georgia, except it is from an African American family's perspective. Retelling some of Carter's same remembrances (e.g., of Joe Louis's first heavyweight victory), Andrews's side of the story gives his firsthand accounts of how his family struggled as sharecroppers.

Our whole KCAC teacher team also read books about earlier history in Georgia, specifically about the Cherokees' place in the American Southeast. Two novels we read, Diane Glancy's (1996) *Pushing the Bear* and Robert Conley's (1992) *Mountain Windsong*, retell the stories of the Removal of the Cherokee and the Trail of Tears. As I mentally reviewed the books during my visit to the Paulding County Museum, I realized that though the events they depict occurred in the 19th century, they provided important information about the eventual formation of Georgia farms (e.g., the land lottery). Both novels used historical events and documents as backdrops, creating substantial historical fiction, leading me to realize that these two books could anchor this research project, because the Cherokee had once roamed the lands of Paulding County before the land became farms. It dawned on me that if I could get my students to realize that historical fiction takes true history and shapes it according to the storyteller's perspective, they would see the importance of researching their own community, preserving those stories, and arriving at their own understanding of the community and how it had changed over time.

To begin their awareness, I divided my students into two groups. One group read *Mountain Windsong* (Conley, 1992) and the other group read *Pushing the Bear* (Glancy, 1996). They shared what they learned with one another, so that all my students had some understanding of both books, while only having read one. Meanwhile, my research had to continue, because I wasn't sure that there were enough resources in the public domain for student access. I was not ready for my students to hear about this project until I had done more digging.

After I visited the museum, I ventured onto the Internet and found a Web site for a genealogical society and therein found a way to e-mail the members explaining my project and asking for help in locating information about the Paulding County community—people, local stories, and legends. I received several replies from people all over the Southeast, offering names, titles of books, and even phone numbers and addresses of people I could contact for help. One individual suggested that I use a two-volume set of Judge W. A. Foster's (1983) *Paulding County: Its People and Places*. One person let me know that the local public library had a heritage room. Lynn W. Sylvester of the Paulding County Genealogical Society sent me a list of genealogy Web sites. All these sites provide ways to search for families, ancestry, and roots. Just by sending out one e-mail, I was able to make contact with total strangers who were more than willing to help me in my research of Paulding County.

ESTABLISHING A NEED FOR STUDENT RESEARCH

Now that I had completed my preliminary research, I was ready to share the idea with students. I was teaching a ninth-grade honors class that year, and our school curriculum mandated that all students complete a research project. Perfect!

I explained my own personal community research as well as the KCAC project to my students, leaving out my disappointing experience at the Paulding County Museum. I did not want to shape their opinions; nor did I want to cramp their research. They needed to make their own discoveries, minus my prejudices. Amazingly enough, I realized that they were intrigued by a teacher who had actually done an activity before assigning it to students. In an effort to keep the project flexible (remember, they were freshmen), I allowed my students to do more general, wide-ranging research on the community, rather than focusing just on its rural heritage. Also, by keeping the project broad, they would develop a sense of community through their own self-directed research—*I hoped*. As I introduced the community-based research project to my freshmen, I established the framework by asking five questions:

1. What do you know about your school?
2. What do you know about your community?
3. What do you know about your county?
4. Why should you know this information?
5. Why should this knowledge make a difference to you?

Some of my students' responses to these questions were as follows:

- "My knowledge of the community is low. I can't blame this on not growing up in Paulding County because I moved here when I was 6. It may be because many teachers knew little on the subject and never passed it on to others. This information could be useful in that you can understand where older people of the county come from. I could know what they had been through and things like that." (Ricky)
- "My community is a very friendly and traditional environment. . . . [It is] one of the fastest growing counties, but . . . true southern traditions still remain intact." (Kelly)

- "Knowing this information gives me a sense of belonging." (Chase)
- "I like knowing where I am from because it gives me a rich knowledge of where I live." (Holly)
- "I know that a long time ago when we drew up the map of Georgia why the counties are so small compared to other states. I believe this is because of an old law stating that a person should be able to walk to the main city such as Dallas to Paulding County. Remember, they didn't have cars when they mapped Georgia." (Ricky)

Ricky's point was valid. Traveling through Georgia's county seats, I have seen perfect examples of what he said. Because of a need for communication, county seats were designed for accessibility. With these questions and answers, I was able to justify the need for my community-based research project. I was not sure whether my students actually saw the need for community research (rather than just seeking a grade); however, I hoped that many would embrace it once they began their initial background work.

DEFINING TERMS TO PROMOTE DIALOGUE

To begin the community research project, I had my students define three pivotal terms: *community*, *heritage*, and *culture*. I chose these terms because I felt that if my students were to grasp the need for community research, they needed to examine words associated with what a community is—culture, heritage, then community. If we were to understand the guiding principle behind our project, these definitions were crucial. I wanted my students to grasp the importance of community while forming an appreciation of their own heritage and developing a tolerance for all cultures.

After we defined those terms, students were directed to pair up with a partner, each member of the pair interviewing the other, learning everything from complete name to parents to grandparents to ethnicity. For some, these answers were not possible until they had had the opportunity to go home and talk with their parents or grandparents, establishing communication with the home; thus, parents/grandparents learned about our project, too.

As straightforward as these activities appear, I created a dialogue within my classroom, establishing an environment in which students felt comfortable discussing their backgrounds, their cultures, and their communities. Even my students who have lived in Paulding County all their lives learned information from one another. Also, new students became a part of the classroom community because after this activity they did not have to be introduced or feel as though they had to answer inquiring questions from others.

Attempting to facilitate students' synthesizing of the acquired information, I asked them to think critically about what they could do to make their communal space in the world more tolerant and understanding of others' differences. In an essay, students answered the following question:

> What do you think can be done to create a more unified community? This question should be considered on the following levels: individual, family, this classroom, school, and community.

Students had the choice of writing on each of these items or focusing on one level. No matter which direction they chose, students realized that the central focus of their essay was to offer solutions—the how-to—of creating a more unified community.

Getting my students to realize the importance of looking at our community through different perspectives elicited diverse responses on many different levels. Many of the students looked at the community as a whole and wanted to see it blend culturally diverse families; in other words, they wanted to have one community only, not divided by race, class, or ethnicity. On another level, the writing activity caused some students to examine their own prejudices, forcing them to seek solutions to an age-old problem. Their responses and open discussions created an atmosphere of respect for themselves, their classmates, their communities, their heritage, and their cultures.

The excerpts from two student essays below provide examples of my students' varied opinions:

> To unify ourselves, we need to be open to new, fresh ideas such as joining youth groups, participating in community service projects, and various other activities in the community. By joining in with a positive outlook, we can discover exactly who we are as individuals, and we can begin to venture down the long and gratifying road called life. . . . To consolidate our families, we need to be compassionate and supportive toward one another, and we need to try and spend as much quality time together as possible. Family projects and outings are very positive things that we should all try and do at least once or twice a month. . . . Together we can make a difference, and it starts with a single individual with the ambition and the heart to change a society. (Rebecca)

Rebecca's response looked good on the surface, but it still did not take into account nontraditional families of our times. How could I get my students to realize that not all families are alike? Communities are diverse in more than just ethnicity, and I needed my students to understand this important fact.

> If we get the idea we can be mean to people and still unify the community, we are utterly wrong. If we, as individuals, changed the way we think to incorporate other feelings, it would make unification of the community a lot easier. . . . Unifying the community has a lot to do with being less selfish and at least considering the consequences of our actions. All the people of the community need to . . . respect and care for their friends. (Michael)

Michael's response probably came closer to what I was seeking originally. He made direct statements but failed to explain how a community could be less selfish. If people were selfish, what were they being selfish about? He could have answered this question, and then he could have offered his solution.

After reading their essays, I noted that many of the students were already beginning to place an importance on unifying a community; but more important, they were realizing that our classroom should be the beginning. Along with presenting observations about unity in the community, they raised questions and offered some suggestions, but many did not reach the point I was hoping for. As the teacher and facilitator of this project, I wanted my students to become fighters for justice or proactive citizens, seeking to create a more unified community outside the classroom; however, I needed to keep in mind that this project was not going to change their lives immediately.

STUDENTS RESEARCHING COMMUNITY SPACES

As the school year progressed, students were given the final piece of the project—the actual community research assignment. Because I led my students through the initial steps to community research, they were ready to begin the actual research thoughtfully instead of jumping into it before they were ready. They had a complete understanding of community within the classroom, they had established communication with their families, and they had begun to discover the importance of preserving history as well as embracing change.

To begin our list of places to research, I wrote *churches* on the board, and then asked for more ideas. Students eagerly made their suggestions, and eventually we had compiled an extensive list: churches, barns and other agricultural structures, recreation, restaurants, shopping, government complexes, town squares, school buildings and histories, historic landmarks, county fairs, industry, arts/crafts, historic figures, or roads/ development. Divided into groups, students were told to select from the list of ideas. While the list seemed to be never-ending, it gave students a variety of choices, hopefully helping them tap into something of interest, and I had enough ideas for three classes.

This research project had a twofold component: It was both written and visual. Students had to write a paper in an I-Search format, revealing all information found; and working in teams, they had to create a visual product (e.g., photographs, videotape) for class presentation. The I-Search format contained investigative questions regarding their topics. I wanted the class to examine the past and present of each category, locating the information via personal interviews with relatives and community members, further establishing our connection with the greater community area. The visual component could involve something as simple as a trifold board or as elaborate as a video. For instance, a group studying recreation created a picture album, complete with pictures of local parks and recreation sites. I did not want to be too specific with the visual component, because I wanted the students to use their creativity instead of replicating the same visual for each group. I wanted variety and I got variety.

The final projects often centered on family stories—a special tree on family property where family reunions are held; local development; a father's involvement with the Black school in the community. Lisa, who researched local cemeteries, contacted the Paulding County Historical Society and joined. Intrigued by the project, members invited her to participate on the Cemetery Committee, and her mother spent an entire schoolday driving Lisa around to make pictures of the local cemeteries. The first cemetery that they visited is located just outside Dallas, the county seat of Paulding. The cemetery has rolling hills with markers decorating those hills. Many of the markers show obvious signs of aging; however, their looming size reminded me of a passing tradition, compared to what exists in the cemeteries of today. After visiting this rather historical cemetery, Lisa and her mother visited smaller ones along the sides of the roads, always located near small churches that seem to have existed since the beginning of Paulding County. One particular cemetery is located across from New Hope Baptist Church, which happens to be connected to the

Civil War. Historical markers in the area tell the story of how a battle was fought on that ground, making it hallowed.

One of my favorite projects involved prominent families. Those students found that four families were dominant in Paulding County stories, so they focused their research on them. Each student in the group took one family, found someone to interview, and captured a story, complete with pictures. Also, they included information about where these families had come from as well as a basic family tree for each family.

Another group in my class researched a local produce market located just around the corner from their neighborhood. This team was not from Paulding County, and they did not have a direct interest in local history, so they asked me if they could interview a farmer who works right now at this local market and make a documentary from the interview. I acquiesced, and they produced a video that captured the essence of the farmer and his business.

Having the students research their community spaces brought a sense of closure to this project; but more than anything else, my students enjoyed it. On the last day of presentations, we had a class picnic and students brought southern-style food (fried chicken, coleslaw, macaroni and cheese, green beans, biscuits, chocolate cake, lemon pie, and sweet iced tea) to celebrate their heritage. The students obviously enjoyed the day, and they did not want the final bell to ring. Each project was displayed, so that we were surrounded by work from all the classes, and while we ate, everyone saw the complete research project. In essence, we had created our own community museum, and students enjoyed having the opportunity to examine the display boards as well as to appreciate what their community held for them.

ANALYSIS AND IMPLICATIONS

The community-based research project allowed me to veer away from the normal English research paper, which many students and teachers dread. It allowed my students to do valid research, involving their community— where they live. What do people really know about their communities? We live in a society where people constantly move, rarely taking the time to leisurely stroll, speak to neighbors, or examine the local museum. Through this project, my students had to slow down . . . talk with people . . . ask questions . . . find answers about things that books really could not provide for them. Also, this project involved having my students take ownership.

Will I do this project again? Of course! I believe in my community and I want my students (all my students) to believe in it, too. I cannot think of a better way to convince them than having them do community research. With each year, I have added to the project or changed it, giving my students an opportunity to see that writers do edit their work and that it's OK to make changes. In fact, having moved to another growing rural community north of Paulding, I have taken this project with me to my new school.

We—our community, our heritage, our culture—come from the richness of the stories told and retold, and realizing the importance of these stories requires that they be captured and preserved, much like Whitman's opening lines of this chapter. The stories are there, just like the grass under our boots. When we ask, we find them.

REFERENCES

Andrews, R. (1990). *The last radio baby*. Atlanta: Peachtree Publishers.

Carter, J. (2000). *An hour before daylight: Memories of a rural boyhood*. New York: Simon & Schuster.

Conley, R. J. (1992). *Mountain windsong*. Norman: University of Oklahoma Press.

Foster, W.A., Jr. (1983). *Paulding County: Its people and places. Vol. I and II*. Roswell, GA: W. H. Wolfe Assoc.

Glancy, D. (1996). *Pushing the bear: A novel of the Trail of Tears*. New York: Harcourt Brace.

Miller, C. (1933). *Lamb in his bosom*. New York:Harper.

Vizenor, G. (1998). *Fugitive poses: Native American scenes of absence and presence*. Lincoln: University of Nebraska Press.

CHAPTER 4

A City Too Busy to Reflect?
Public History, Controversy,
and Civic Engagement

LeeAnn Lands

In 1981, Gary Trudeau captured an America (and a military) seeking to escape the past when he penned character Mike Doonesbury watching the news on television. An army general being interviewed declared, "It's time we moved forward and finally put the conflict in Southeast Asia behind us!"

The reporter responded, "Excuse me, General, but aside from your personal convenience, why would you have people 'put behind them' precisely those things which should never be forgotten?" The reporter prodded, "Tell me, General, is it all right for the Japanese to be 'sick and tired of Pearl Harbor'? Should the Germans ever be allowed to 'put the Holocaust behind them'?"

"Yes," the general explained, "they're allies."

"And the Nuremberg trials?" the reporter posed.

"Wallowing in World War II," the general retorted (Trudeau, 1981).

While Trudeau depicted a military tired of answering for transgressions in Vietnam, his cartoon also reflected a larger, public reluctance to engage difficult historical or policy-related issues. Similarly, many students view discussion of controversial topics as antithetical to the goal of establishing "community." Such discussions, the reasoning goes, provoke animosity, reintroduce old hurts, or sometimes erect new barriers. Rather, many students, like Trudeau's general, would prefer to "move on." Yet communities benefit not only from citizens who are open to discussing and working through various contentious public issues and past events,

but also from members who are willing to facilitate such exchange responsibly, encouraging mutual respect and understanding between community members. As historian Patricia Mooney-Melvin (1999) asserts:

> Students' lack of historical knowledge about the past results in an inability
> to see themselves, their families, and their communities as part of the larger
> process of American history. If students fail to see their own histories as
> important, they do not believe that they can have an impact on their envi-
> ronments. (p. 17)

Adopting this framework, I decided to add to Kennesaw State
University's introductory public history course a component that would
move beyond the usual readings-based discussion of how professionals
tackled sensitive issues. I devised a project that would walk students
through ways to facilitate such dialogue with the public. In addition to
giving the students usable professional skills, I sought to promote civic
engagement, to support students in proactively taking these lessons out
into their noncollege worlds. In our fall 2001 class, I charged students
with designing an exhibit that would encourage our northwest Georgia
community to explore its history of race relations and the subculture surrounding lynching—an exhibit that would help build community by
facilitating the *public's* exploration of our nation's (and region's) violent
past.

The project was informed by principles and practices espoused by the
Keeping and Creating Communities (KCAC) project, specifically that collaboration is essential to keeping and creating communities; that there is
value in recovering and critiquing community texts; and that shared actions contribute to the formation of community cultures. The project also
developed out of my conviction that historians (public or academic) should
advance *public* discussion about the state of their community, nation, or
world. I wanted our students not only to be willing participants in such
community formation, but also to be willing to lead the charge.

Public history is, generally speaking, history geared toward nonacademic
audiences. It includes history as interpreted through museums or exhibitions, along with archival management and historic preservation. It involves
the study of public commemoration such as historical markers, as well as
nontraditional forms of public interpretation of historical events such
as plays or walking tours (Cole, 1994). Public-history classes and programs train students to pursue these fields professionally and to view the
public-historical landscape critically, looking for larger meanings, political uses of history, the development of collective memory, and equitable
representation. In my classroom, for example, and following historian

James Loewen's (1999) model, we asked, "Whose history makes it onto our state historical markers?"

The introduction to public-history class is required for those students pursuing the public-history undergraduate certificate at Kennesaw State and is an elective for history majors and minors. Otherwise, the class is open to all students who have completed the general education requirement, U.S. history since 1890. The class reflects the school's population, which is predominantly White, suburban, and lower-middle to middle income. These residents of an area long stereotyped as a destination for 1970s "White flight" proved to be an interesting population with whom to try out community-based examination of sensitive issues by using the KCAC teaching model. Additionally, through their prior formal and informal education experiences, many of the students seemed to have been acculturated to avoid social controversy or to negotiate through it with a "southern" brand of politeness. But I envisioned using public history as a way to encourage and facilitate more direct engagement with social issues.

Controversy is a topic examined in most public-history programs. Recall the arguments over the proposed *Enola Gay* exhibit at the National Air and Space Museum, an exhibit that eventually—after pressure from veterans' groups, political organizations, and consequently the funding agencies—was so modified from its original design that the original framework was canned (Wallace, 1996a; Miller, 1995). As recently as April 2003, protests erupted over the exhibition *Mirroring Evil* at the Jewish Museum (New York), which included 13 artists' work based on the Holocaust. Indeed, history is personal; it is part of how we view *ourselves*. Hence, the ability to confront and work through sensitive issues with multiple interest groups is relevant to all our students. To address two key elements—reflecting on other agencies' handling of controversy and proactively examining a sensitive issue—I developed a multidimensional course segment grounded in KCAC learning strategies that any teacher can adapt to different topics or student populations.

This Community and Controversy component was one of the last I scheduled us to cover. The students needed grounding in basic public history concepts (the functions of public history, memory, exhibit design and critique, and so on) before they would fully understand why some topics might be controversial. They needed to be comfortable with thinking about public history and the variety of approaches that different groups, regions, and even countries have taken to interpreting the past. Likewise, they needed exposure to the politics of public history, the lack of curatorial freedom, and the power of funding bodies.

My students' aversion to introducing controversial topics within the classroom (much less the larger community) was evident early in the course, making this segment all the more important. This hesitancy, in part, was caused by their lack of experience with discussion. In this class, most sessions focused on discussing group projects or reflecting on the previous class's field trip. Because most other history classes in the college used lecture, the students needed time to get acclimated to the seminar method. It seemed, however, that the students did not feel comfortable disagreeing with one another. I observed eye-rolls by some students when others offered opinions contrary to their own, but rarely a verbal challenge. Outside class, students were more willing to discuss contrary opinions with me, but when asked why they didn't bring up those points in class, some expressed reluctance to cause ill feelings.

When I realized that students were reluctant to offer challenging arguments, we collectively examined the idea of "discussion" and the ideology behind the "seminar method" of teaching. The students concurred that this was a useful form of learning and knowledge development, but they still didn't disagree. In fact, most wrote strong papers about such topics as the mythologizing of the Old South or the narrow portrayal of women's lives in a particular local exhibit. But they balked at "live" discussion over contentious issues. This didn't bode well for the Community and Controversy segment of the course.

CONTROVERSY BEGINS AT HOME

The mounting of *Without Sanctuary*, a collection of lynching photographs assembled by Atlantan James Allen, presented a unique opportunity for my Community and Controversy segment. By engaging with primary materials used for the exhibit—available through *journalE*, an online multimedia journal (www.journale.com/withoutsanctuary)—and planning their own exhibit of the lynching images, students would collectively pursue the meaning of the events and materials *themselves* while at the same time considering how to facilitate this discussion with the larger community. The images of lynching—vigilante justice visited most often upon Black males, but also on Jews, Catholics, women, and other groups—are disturbing enough, but Allen's collection impresses upon viewers the larger culture surrounding such expressions of power and hatred. After all, many of Allen's images are *postcards*—images sent to friends and relatives, or tacked on a wall to fondly recall a particular place or event. Worse, many of the images suggest a carnival atmosphere. Crowds gather.

Families are present. Young girls are seen posing next to a hanging. The questions such images raise are innumerable. They sadden, shock, and repulse.

The contextual material was intellectually accessible to my students, an element I actively sought for a case study. I've found that presenting students with a combination of new content *and* new methodology is troublesome. If students are comfortable with particular historical content, they can concentrate on new methodology, and vice versa. In this case, our history students were already familiar with the history of race relations in the South, lynching, Jim Crowism, and their legacy. Through conversations, I found out that most students were familiar with Atlanta's history of image-consciousness and, too, they were aware of just how embedded issues of race remain in southern culture. Since we had a familiar content area, we could focus more fully on methods for developing community dialogue.

GETTING STARTED

Throughout the first 8 to 10 weeks of our introductory class, students explored approaches to bringing history to the public. On in-class field trips, we did not normally follow the standard tourist tour, but visited with curators, collectors, association directors, archivists, and the like, who discussed various hurdles they confronted and even their own impression of the field's mission. We checked out the grassroots preservation efforts at Prater's Mill in Varnell, Georgia; discussed the trials of starting and operating a historical society with the director of Roswell's historical association; and chatted with the director of Sloss Furnaces (in Birmingham, Alabama) about innovative labor education programs, as well as the challenges of raising funds to stabilize the national landmark. In out-of-class assignments, students visited sites "as tourists"—viewing the site as would any other visitor. They followed up by reflecting on these sites in writing and often discussing them in class. By the time we were scheduled to start Community and Controversy, the students had completed two exhibit reviews, gone on a variety of field trips, and read a number of scholarly and popular pieces critiquing exhibits, memorials, oral history projects, and the like. Additionally, they'd already been through two in-class workshops designing their own "exhibits" on different topics, so they were comfortable with being given a task, brainstorming solutions, developing consensus, and summarizing their results. In one in-class assignment, for example, the group was charged with proposing two designs for a public exhibit examining the history of Kennesaw State University since the school's founding in 1963, and explaining each design. Thus, with some practice at developing their own ideas and working as a public-history team, they were ready to pursue more complex issues.

The first component of the Community and Controversy segment was the reading of specific case studies on how other agencies had handled curating exhibits on controversial material. We read and discussed historian Mike Wallace's (1996a) essay "The Battle of the *Enola Gay*," a critical assessment of the National Air and Space Museum's unintended participation in the 1990s culture wars; Wallace's (1996b) article "Disney's America," which summarizes the squall the Walt Disney Company created when it announced its intention to open a new theme park tracing America's history; historian Debra Michals's (2001) essay "Did the Women's Museum Wimp Out?" a scathing critique of the whitewashing of "sensitive" material through pressure applied by corporate sponsors; and Jeffrey Gettleman's (2000) recent newspaper article on the protests that erupted after the placement of a Nathan Bedford Forrest monument in a predominantly African American neighborhood in Selma, Alabama. In the following class, I presented our project: to design an exhibit plan based on James Allen's lynching photograph and postcard collection.

PLANNING OUR EXHIBIT

To the class, I introduced the collection and pointed out that it had already been publicly exhibited in New York and Pittsburgh. Now Allen wanted to bring it home—to Atlanta. I explained that mounting such a project might sound easy, but the proposal had already generated much discussion, discussion that we were going to visit and engage in ourselves. We sought to create a dialogue with the community about our city's and region's past history of racial violence and, in turn, to confront its legacy. By hashing out the meaning of this difficult material as a group (and presumably with the public), we would be forging new communities of understanding. We'd be collectively finding meaning in the past. Indeed, before class had begun for the semester, the *Atlanta Journal-Constitution* (AJC) had framed the debate for metro Atlantans. An August 2001 article outlined "the squabble" mounting over James Allen's and John Littlefield's proposed exhibit (Fox, 2001b). Rick Beard, then director of the Atlanta History Center, signaled his reluctance when he suggested that such an exhibit tour through several *other* cities before coming to Atlanta. The *AJC* went on to quote Beard's explanation that "put bluntly, the 'city too busy to hate' is often also the city too busy to think deeply about the painful aspects of its past until somebody 'foreign' tells them it is OK and perhaps even important to do so" (Fox, 2001a, p. E1).

Because *journalE* had curated a stripped-down, Web-based exhibit of the material, my class had a collection to work with. We ignored the interpretive material that supplemented the online collection and focused on the primary material. (Later we discussed how we could use that secondary material to enhance the public's understanding). And we discussed the exhibit plans as if we were, in reality, planning for an actual exhibit. Because the course is not designed to provide rigorous training for future museologists, we focused on the *planning process* of determining the interpretive approach, media mix, and public-forum elements.

After warning students about the harrowing nature of the images, I took them through the collection online. We looked at approximately 35 images and read where the lynching had taken place, any background the collector knew about the crime at hand, and what (if any) text had been added to the image or postcard. Except for the occasional "What does that say?" we didn't talk while viewing the material for the first time. We then held a brief, open discussion that mostly consisted of particular things that stood out to the students. Students commented on gender and regional representation, the nature of the text on the postcards, the different forms lynching took, and the like. After this initial discussion, we went through the material again.

We considered whether we, in our newly formed (if virtual) agency, were really willing to host such an exhibit. What could be gained? Like many Atlantans, some of my students were reluctant to commit themselves to launching such an exhibit; they were afraid that the city wasn't ready to confront its past. We went on to discuss what gave people that impression, and the students struggled to articulate specific examples. Some cited the continued use of Confederate symbols throughout the region while others offered personal anecdotes of some locals' use of violence as a scare tactic. One student, for example, told of a neighbor standing in his yard with a gun when an African American couple moved into the neighborhood. In contrast, those students arguing for the exhibit were so moved by this new material (like most who see Allen's photographs), and how it surpassed the now-tired textbook depictions of the Jim Crow South, that they felt others would be intellectually challenged by it, that it was a "public service" to bring the exhibit to fruition.

In a significant act, Emory University (the institution that was temporarily holding the collection) and the Atlanta History Center held two public forums to gauge opinion about mounting such an exhibit—inviting the community directly into the discussion (Fox, 2000a, p. 1F; Fox, 2000b, p. 1D). The sessions were not just well attended, but full in a number of ways. The forums indicated just how important the regional population considered the healing and community-building that could be possible through such public exhibits. At the same time, Emory and the Atlanta History Center sent the message that they viewed themselves as members of the community, participants in our region's cultural development, and not "ivory tower" establishments set to dictate history to the less well informed. We read the newspaper reports, and they rendered clear just how important the discussion of our collective past was for many people. Seeing this public record made the students—at least initially—more comfortable mounting the controversial material.

Back at our virtual exhibit, we needed to develop a mission statement. This tends to be a cumbersome idea, so we approached it by developing, first, a list of questions we wanted answered by the exhibit. Questions included, Who did these things? Who were the bystanders? Why was Allen collecting such things? What were his goals? Why wasn't the established legal system in play? Who were the victims? What was the socioeconomic structure of the area in which this had occurred? Why is the South over-represented? These and other questions went toward the task of developing our tentative themes:

1. What is lynching?
2. Who were the victims?
3. Who were the perpetrators?
4. What was the economic and cultural context for the events?
5. What was the subculture surrounding lynching?

We then sought to firmly articulate our mission: to educate the public about violence, lynching, and racial and ethnic tensions since the 1880s and to provoke a response so as to create greater understanding between people of different races and ethnicities. We proceeded to discuss what general spatial design would support these themes. We also started thinking about *how* to interpret the material or answer the questions they posed: Would it be a stripped-down exhibit with larger-than-life copies of the images? Would there be a tape-recorder tour? Would there be background information on lynching, violence, and the like?

I followed with asking which of the ideas presented or talked about the students had liked. One student had mentioned a depiction of a slave ship that had been installed at the *Africa: One Continent, Many Worlds* exhibition at Fernbank Museum of Natural History here in Atlanta. The visitor walked through a passage with lighting that gave the effect that one was in the hold of a moving ship. At the same time, sounds of Africans (presumably in the hold with you, stolen, sick, confused, and angry) were piped in from all directions. The students latched on to this immersion, "experiential" element immediately. How to pull it off? They noted that some of the most awe-inspiring of Allen's photos were those of large crowds viewing a lynching, so they decided to enlarge crowd photographs to life size, and wallpaper a small room with them, as if the crowds were surrounding whoever was in the room. Then they'd install a tree in one end of the room, as if it was really growing there, roots protruding through the floor and canopy going through the ceiling. The tree would have a noose on it. Then they'd introduce the stereo sound element, not simply with the sounds of a crowd, but audio that indicated the carnival atmosphere, including laughter, jeering, and children's voices. Within the room, they'd provide simple bench seating to facilitate extended reflection for those who wished it. They had no desire to depict the death itself, but the sense of being in the large crowd, part of the atmosphere of the day. They wanted it to be "haunting." They wanted the viewers to take this experience away with them.

Planning the principal section of the exhibit was more contentious. Which photos do we use? What kind of interpretation do we add? Do we lead the viewer to a certain conclusion (making a closed-end argument as a historian does in a paper), or do we present these events from multiple angles and leave the interpretation more to the viewer? Our class was divided on these standard curatorial dilemmas, some preferring to let viewers draw their own conclusions, others insisting that the historian's role was to sift through the muck and then tell the viewer what conclusions had been drawn. After all, the latter group reasoned, the visitor doesn't have time to view all the primary material available—they depend on the museum curators to help sort out the issues.

I took the students' ideas and, before the next class, developed a first-draft exhibit layout, attempting to incorporate the elements that seemed most important to the group and to find an interpretive middle ground. Overall, the proposal adopted a minimalist framework. Four large, two-sided panels, set centrally in our exhibit space, would give general information on lynching, including numbers per year, states where they occurred, and the like. Lining the walls would be a selection of the lynching postcards, showing both sides of each. In a double-sided panel set in front of each wall, two postcards would be featured. In those cases, more information would be given on the background of the victim, the alleged crime, and any other information known about what was going on. Here, the students wanted to indicate the sheer number of deaths that had occurred in this manner by having many photographs mounted on the exterior walls. By eliminating the overt interpretive element, the intensity of the photographs and number would make the statement. At the same time, the students recognized that viewers would want to know *why* these events really were occurring. In that case, the featured postcards would provide more detail, suggesting the vigilante nature of the act and reiterating the carnival nature of the events. I mocked up the exhibit layout in PowerPoint (see Figure 4.1).

Particular questions being presented in the "real-life" debate were also fleshed out in our alternative universe. When an Atlanta History Center board member was quoted in the paper as suggesting that an academic institution would be a more appropriate setting for such an exhibit, we discussed the implications of that statement. Naturally this led to where we would install our exhibit. Just who were *our* potential viewers? Whom did we expect to attend, and whom did we *want* to attend? Adopting the board member's suggestion, some promoted mounting the exhibit at an academic institution (such as Emory), which had

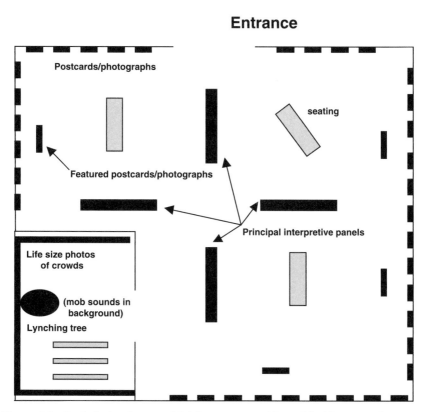

Figure 4.1. Draft design for an exhibit layout created by public history students.

the advantage of drawing on a more "astute" audience that would "understand the context" in which these events took place. Others promoted a more accessible venue, which they equated with a more accessible history. Often, as we moved on to these questions, we had to revisit our mission statement, our original goals, whom we'd sought to serve, what ideas we'd sought to advance. Our mission, which had sounded so grand—"to advance understanding between people of different races and ethnicities"—was in danger of becoming watered down in the face of fears of disorder, anger, and tension that continued to resurface.

We concluded the Community and Controversy segment by discussing what other exhibits we could mount that might assist the public in examining sensitive policy or cultural issues. One student suggested that we examine our university's growth and environmental policies since the institution's founding—issues that have produced strong reactions from students, faculty, staff, and the local community. After a few rounds on that topic, the students decided they wouldn't go through with the proposal, given the current "political climate" on campus. Asked why they thought they couldn't host a program that examined the ramifications of the university's spatial expansion into local neighborhoods or the declining green space (all topics the students had raised), some responded that the university rarely sought student input, which suggested that discussion wasn't welcome. A few thought such programming moot, as they suspected that the administration wouldn't take their views seriously. Alas, we still have some work to do to encourage student engagement—even in the most immediate community of their university—along with trust that such involvement would be welcome.

I decided that other relevant elements would be addressed in more depth in future semesters, because I had failed in this initial effort to allocate enough time to explore how we could directly interact with the public *within* the exhibit. The curator of the real exhibit, Joseph Jordan, didn't miss this feature, though. When it opened in April 2002 in a contextualized setting at the Martin Luther King, Jr., Center, Atlanta's *Without Sanctuary* exhibit included a "Reflect and Respond Room" that invited the public to react to the photographs and postcards on paper or online. Likewise, *journalE*'s exhibit incorporated a forum element that invited response and reflection.

ANALYSIS AND IMPLICATIONS

In future classes, I plan to introduce an element that will explicitly walk students through the practice of polite disagreement. It was apparent that students needed to learn how to constructively disagree among themselves and to learn to use this disagreement to advance project development and learning. Such exercises will make students more comfortable with addressing sensitive issues.

Controversial topics are difficult for professional public historians to tackle, much less junior and senior undergraduates. Yet whether acting as museologists, nonprofit managers, or preservationists or simply acting out their role as citizen, students will confront volatile issues. Historic preservationists, for example, are often called upon to assist downtown development authorities or preservation commissions in negotiating the establishment of preservation ordinances. This is a mediation role in which the preservationist is expected to negotiate terms with the larger community, reconciling property owners' needs and historic preservation. Activities can quickly become battlegrounds whose outcomes range from increased tensions to lawsuits.

This civic skills–building project is also applicable beyond public history. Our communities of northwest Georgia, for example, have a range of public issues to sort through, from the acrimonious debates surrounding the building of the "Northern Arc"—a pricey second interstate bypass that would initially ease traffic congestion, but potentially pull the metropolitan area further into the hinterland—to the region's changing ethnic communities. Similarly, our citizens have ample opportunities to renegotiate understandings of our national history. As historian Mike Wallace has persistently asked, where are our exhibits analyzing the Vietnam War? Or urban renewal? (1996c, p. 120; Wallace, 1996d, p. 47). To look to for guidance, we have bold experiments examining culture and power, such as Columbia University's exhibit *Stonewall and Beyond: Lesbian and Gay Culture* and *Holding the Rock*, an innovative interpretation of the 1969 Indian seizure of Alcatraz Island, curated by the National Park Service (Strange & Loo, 2001).

While we have these innovative exhibits to look to, they are far too rare, a situation that narrows our students' knowledge base and appears to limit creative thinking. In retrospect, it is clear that the students in the class who had been exposed to more cultural programming (not just museums, but also theater, art, and even dance) and over a broader geographical area (e.g., New York City, the Southwest) brought more and varied approaches to our project. However, since I had not expected significant differences to surface, I failed to measure cultural-programming exposure before class started. Study of this variable will no doubt reveal rich data in the next round. (Correlations between race or social class and exposure to cultural resources could not be measured in this particular group, given the all-White and largely homogenous socioeconomic makeup of the enrollment; future courses' student populations may prove more diverse in this regard, as the university's compostion is changing).

My students appeared to be fairly accepting of the idea that public exhibits could be used to foster understanding, historical context, and the building of community. Generally speaking, the history profession promotes the belief that historical understanding is *relevant* to policy making and to one's role as a citizen, so this was no surprise. The students also concurred that we could use the public forum and exhibits to nurture community. That said, members of this particular class remained uncomfortable with *risk*, brought home by the fact that we were "virtually mounting" an exhibit at the same time as the "real" exhibit was being planned. The fact that we were discussing how we would handle this exhibit proposal while similar debates were being held a few miles down the road gave the exercise more validity. Would we really mount such horrific images in a *very* public place? What would the outcome be? Would we be creating community and understanding, or breaking them down? Indeed, this reluctance to take risk was what I sought to chip away.

The students' reaction mirrors the larger public stance. As Wallace (1996b) points out, many people consider museums to be "irrelevant," simply sites of pleasant recreational activities that might generate tourism dollars (p. 167). Yet historian Howard Zinn (2001) has long promoted history as "the work of a citizen," averring that "in a world hungry for solutions, we ought to welcome the emergence of the historian . . . as an activist-scholar, who thrusts himself and his works into the crazy mechanism of history, on behalf of values in which he deeply believes. This makes of him more than a scholar; it makes him a citizen in the ancient Athenian sense of the word" (p. 203). And Wallace (1996c) recently implored museum directors and curators to "become partners with communities in effecting change" and to use museums and programs "as centers of civic debate and organization" (p. 128). Many museums have answered that call, such as in the New York Public Library's *Garbage! The History and Politics of Trash in New York City,* which not only looked at trash historically, but also included suggestions for responsibly restructuring consumption.

In this first run of the Community and Controversy project, focusing on *Without Sanctuary* was all the more challenging because the real-life debate was being played out in our own community. The students were intimately familiar with the cultural issues inherent in broaching the topic of race relations and violence. They knew the controversy. And now they'd walked through confronting it. Indeed, perhaps what will ultimately help ease students through future risk-taking forums will be the fact that Atlantans "took the risk," and it worked.

REFERENCES

Cole, Jr., C. C. (1994). Public history: What difference has it made? *Public Historian 16*, 11.

Fox, C. (2000a, December 8). Lynching exhibit draws support. *Atlanta Journal-Constitution*, p. 1F.

Fox, C. (2000b, December 6). Share ideas on lynching exhibition. *Atlanta Journal-Constitution*, p. 1D.

Fox, C. (2001a, August 1). Images too painful to see? *Atlanta Journal-Constitution*, p. E1.

Fox, C. (2001b, August 30). Lynching photos get go ahead. *Atlanta Journal-Constitution*, p. 1F.

Gettleman, J. (2000, October 22). To mayor, it's Selma's statue of limitations. *Los Angeles Times*, p. A1.

Loewen, J. W. (1999). *Lies across America: What our historic sites get wrong*. New York: Touchstone.

Michals, D. (2001, June/July). Did the women's museum wimp out? *Ms.*, 58–67.

Miller, P. P. (1995). Smithsonian's Enola Gay exhibit attacked; OAH responds. *NCC Washington Update, 1*, 1.

Mooney-Melvin, P. (1999). Professional historians and the challenge of redefinition. In J. B. Gardner & P. S. LaPaglia (Eds.), *Public history: Essays from the field* (pp. 5–12). Malabar, FL: Krieger.

Strange, C., & Loo, T. (2001). Holding the rock: The Indianization of Alcatraz Island, 1969–1999. *Public Historian, 23*, 55–74.

Trudeau, G. B Cartoon. (1981). Reprinted in (1986), Susan Porter Benson, Stephen Brier, and Roy Rosenzweig (Eds.), *Presenting the past: Essays on history and the public* (p. 3). Philadelphia: Temple University Press.

Wallace, M. (1996a). The battle of the *Enola Gay*. In *Mickey Mouse: History and other essays on American memory* (pp. 269–318). Philadelphia: Temple University Press.

Wallace, M. (1996b). Disney's America. In *Mickey Mouse: History and other essays on American memory* (pp. 159–174). Philadelphia: Temple University Press.

Wallace, M. (1996c). Museums and controversy. In *Mickey Mouse: History and other essays on American memory* (pp. 115–129). Philadelphia: Temple University Press.

Wallace, M. (1996d). Razor ribbons, history museums, and civic salvation. In *Mickey Mouse: History and other essays on American memory* (pp. 33–54). Philadelphia: Temple University Press.

Zinn, H. (2001). *On history*. New York: Seven Stories Press.

CHAPTER 5

Uncovering a Region's Past to Build Community Today: Collaborative Learning About Cherokee Heritage

Patsy Hamby

I live and teach in Paulding County, one of the 10 fastest-growing regions in the nation. As new residents settle in our community of Hiram, our school population is becoming more diverse. Our school district's profile is shifting, and while it still includes a majority of rural, White, middle-income families, an increasing number of our students are children of commuting professionals of diverse ethnicities. Some longtime residents have demonstrated a resistance to the new demographics in our county. In an attempt to keep a small-town atmosphere, some of our city leaders have blocked incentives that would allow major industries to consider moving to our area; for example, the commissioners determine the size of water pipes, a seemingly minor issue, but one that either hampers or promotes growth. I have children of these resisters in my Hiram High School English classroom, where I teach primarily the required 10th-grade literature and composition course. I also have many of the "new arrivals," students whose families typically see Hiram as a bedroom community from which they commute to Atlanta. While not a commuter, I am still a relative newcomer, as several years ago my husband and I moved from the metro Atlanta area to escape the traffic and the continuous noise that accompanies it.

Given my situation of working in a new school in a community that was still new to me, I was a perfect candidate to participate in the Keeping and Creating Communities (KCAC) program. As my colleague in the Kennesaw Mountain Writing Project, Mimi Dyer, began to discuss a grant proposal for KCAC, I was keenly interested because of my goal of helping my students adapt to the changes in our environment and still feel a sense of connectedness to one another and to their families, their school, and their community. I became a participant once the grant had been approved. I reconnected with people I had formerly taught with, particularly Leslie Walker, who had been across the hall from me at my previous school and who now led the team I elected to join as we researched Displaced Heritages, with a focus on the Cherokee Nation.

With the other members of our team, I visited public-history sites such as New Echota, once capital of the Cherokee Nation. On these visits we collected resources to help make the study of Cherokee culture meaningful, both for myself as I participated in the KCAC project's theme-based research and for my students as I eventually would implement materials and concepts from my own research in the classroom. And what a wealth of resources we created.

In my 2nd academic year of the KCAC program, I planned to use my learning about the Cherokee with sophomore World Literature and Composition students, focusing on literature as an avenue for teaching students reflection, collaboration, and strategies for interacting with other cultures. My students could relate to the Cherokee sense of loss and need to rebuild community, I surmised from the previous year's Hiram High research project. A new school, a changing community, and the rich history of our region were the bases for my assumption. As we absorbed the effects of the Atlanta suburban-flight syndrome, we had much to reflect on, research, and preserve, both personally and regionally.

In keeping with KCAC principles, I first determined to "promote community-based inquiry" by making the students aware of the rich history of our community through an examination of the Cherokee Removal before we read Robert Conley's (1992) *Mountain Windsong* and through discussion of the influence of the Cherokee in our region. I felt that all the World Lit students, whether in college or technical prep, whether advanced readers or remedial, could comprehend the advanced and sophisticated culture of the Cherokee and thus relate to the tragic series of events the tribe was forced to endure. I also wished to create a classroom community through "authentic research" and writing as students uncovered their family histories, created an artifact for their own legacy, and shared their findings and creations with the class. With these goals, I developed a collaborative study of Conley's multivocal text, and my efforts were successful beyond my wildest imagination.

TEACHING THE LOST HERITAGE

As I began introducing the Cherokee Removal topic into my curriculum, my first challenge was to determine which literature unit I would focus on to study the Removal with my students. I had several options: one was the nonfiction unit, which in our text includes an excerpt from N. Scott Momaday's (1969/1999) *The Way to Rainy Mountain* in which he discusses the migration of his people, the Kiowa, to what is now Oklahoma. I reasoned that we could compare and contrast the history of the Cherokee and the Kiowa tribes, particularly focusing on their migration experiences. Or I could use one of the several related texts that were required reading for teacher participants in our summer institute, including *Pushing the Bear* (Glancy, 1996) and *Mountain Windsong* (Conley, 1992). For supplementary materials, from my field trips with the KCAC team, I had collected a video titled *The Southeastern Indians* (Couch & Marshall, 1999), which would provide a historical setting for the Removal; a diagram of Cherokee signs and symbols, which I considered for possible connections with art; and ideas for making connections with the text through identifying, reporting, or even creating family artifacts representing family histories.

Some wonderful strategies for projects came from others on the Displaced Heritages team. A middle-school teacher suggested artifacts that the students could create to pass on to descendants: a family tree or a quilt. An elementary teacher offered having the students write their legacies. We found many common threads as we three met with Leslie Walker, our group leader, to discuss approaches for implementation of our theme in the classroom.

As the 2001–2 school year began, I realized that the most practical unit to incorporate the Displaced Heritages theme would be the novel unit, and that I would use *Mountain Windsong* (Conley, 1992). A class set of the novel would be available from KCAC by then. However, as is customary for teachers, I had several constraints with which to contend; one was time to teach the novel and incorporate the background, research, and artifact presentations, since the unit was scheduled in our curriculum as the last one of the year.

Student apathy was another constraint to consider, as I would be teaching the unit to four classes of World Literature and Composition students, most of whom were taking the course as high school sophomores. The course is designated college preparatory, but we offer no alternative course for students considering either immediate employment after high school or attendance at a 2-year technical school. So, since every student is required to take and pass World Lit/Comp, the students would have varied interests and abilities. Our school is not on block scheduling, so I have the students daily for 55-minute classes, and since the novel unit was scheduled shortly before the end of the school year, I knew I would also have the challenge of keeping 16-year-olds engaged when their main agenda was getting the school year over with.

Based on schema theory, my first goal was to provide the students with some historical information on the Cherokee Removal, reviewing facts so the novel would have relevance. I also wished to help those new to the area comprehend the rich history of our geographical region. The long-time residents would be made aware of a history that included the up-rooting of a civilized, well-established culture, the Cherokee; and perhaps they would make connections with other world events and foresee and prevent such actions in the future. Thus, the historical basis for the novel allowed for cross-curricular instruction.

My focus on the Removal would also allow me to address local and state curricular standards. I began with the video *Southeastern Indians* (Couch & Marshall, 1999) and had students complete a response sheet. After the viewing, one student inadvertently complimented me by ex-claiming, "Wow! I didn't know if I was in an English class or a history class!" I also hoped that, as we shared artifacts and discussed the Chero-kee heritage and our own, the students would feel more comfortable with and accepting of one another. This goal was consistent with the charac-ter education mandates for our district, for which our school adopted the theme of Respect. The curriculum standards for language arts were eas-ily met through this unit, as we would definitely read, discuss, and analyze the literature, and the three strands in the novel clearly lend themselves to analyses of tone and point of view. A word list would meet the requirement for study of vocabulary in context and literary terms, and creating the personal written history would meet writing/usage/grammar standards.

BUILDING OUR COMMUNITY

My teaching philosophy includes having students be aware of teacher expectations, and this is accomplished when written instructions and the method of grading are provided, so I gave them a rubric that introduced the five graded assignments and a brief description of each. My students knew from the start that they would be graded for the artifact presenta-tion, completion of the reading logs, activity sheets, the video-viewing guide, and the strand project.

In an attempt to explore our own heritages and to help the students recognize the diversity of our own classroom, I created the first assignment, one that would emphasize research, writing, critical thinking, and oral presentation. For this artifact presentation, I provided the following instructions: Write a description of an artifact or object (a picture, trophy, and so on) that reflects how you see yourself now or that reflects your heritage (minimum three paragraphs). Bring the object and be prepared to read your description and present your object to the class.

I modeled the assignment as I showed the class a dollar bill that my grandmother had given me, and I read a tribute to her that I had previously written, describing how difficult her life had been. I related my mother's comment when she saw what my grandmother had mailed to me: "That will be the hardest-earned dollar you'll ever have."

The sharing of the students' artifacts initiated the creation of our classroom community. Responding to the assignment, some brought copies of their birth certificates, reading where and when they were born and discussing the times they were required to present it as identification. Others brought trophies they had earned in children's athletics, or baby shoes, or pictures of family members. Jenny brought the only picture she had of her father, who was sent to prison in another state shortly after she was born. While she shared, the class was quiet, respectful, and empathetic as she told how she wished to see him again. Indeed, the artifact presentations far exceeded my expectations as an introduction to the Displaced Heritages theme.

To further promote the student buy-in necessary for community-based inquiry, I determined that the students would have choices of reading assignments. Robert Conley, the author of *Mountain Windsong* (1992), ingeniously weaves three genres through the novel, and I determined that these would make logical strands that would allow students to make choices for exploring the theme of Displaced Heritages.

The italicized sections incorporated throughout the novel carry the story of a young boy, Sonny, or "Chooj," learning of his heritage from his grandfather, and this I titled the "Intergenerational" strand. Another clear strand in the novel, written in normal print, carries the love story of two young Cherokee, Oconeechie and Waguli, separated by the Removal, a plot that I termed the "Romantic" strand. The third strand, written in "legalese," presents official documents regarding the Removal, lists and costs of supplies for the march, and other writings of historical significance, and I called this the "Historical" strand.

In the classroom, to give the students a sense of voice and to create interest and a basis for choices, I read several paragraphs from the beginnings of each strand, and I provided note cards and wrote the following instructions on the board:

Select the strand that you prefer, and on the note card, write the following:

A. Your name, date, and period
B. The strand you choose
C. A brief explanation of why you have chosen that strand

I then took the note cards and grouped the students in clusters of three or four; to my surprise (for I felt the students might find the readings of the legal documents rather dry), in each of the four classes, three to four students indicated an interest in the historical section, and so we had a group for each strand. While some of their explanations were quite brief ("I like romantic stories," or "I hate romantic stories"), some were poignant ("The grandfather reminds of how I feel about my own grandpa").

The small reading groups then took on a community relationship of their own as they read their sections. Sometimes one person read aloud to the others, while other groups engaged in silent reading. Again, in order to promote collaboration, I allowed the students to make choices of how they wished to address the readings. All followed the requirements of a 1- to 2-minute daily summary of readings for the class, a reflection in a personal journal, and a record of progress on a daily reading record log to indicate starting and stopping places and to provide one-sentence summaries to enable absentees to catch up.

Students found comfortable reading areas, as some created circles and read seated at their desks or on the floor; others went outside, either in the hallway or to the outdoors just beyond the classroom. I consider choosing their space a primary factor in inviting students to collaboration and inquiry. In reflecting later, I find it cruelly ironic that students were allowed to claim their own space while researching a nation who lost theirs.

On reading days, as the classes entered, the groups picked up folders with their reading logs and summary sheets and settled into their reading groups, while I walked around and monitored progress and clarified information. I spent the most time talking with the historical groups, who had lively discussions of points in the legal documents, particularly about changes in the treaties.

The students never complained about the collaborative assignments as they became engrossed in reading and discussing. While they shared their summaries each day, those working on other strands would ask questions, such as these posed to the historical group: "Where was [Chief] John Ross when the treaty [of 1835] was signed?" and "Who gets the 5 million dollars for Cherokee land?" Such questions between groups gave clear indication of their attention to the way the author was weaving the historical aspects of the Removal and his fictional account of the romantic relationship between the two main characters. The instructional goal of learning through inquiry was achieved, and our community-building process was strengthened along the way. By the end of the unit, students were asking for copies of the novel to read in its entirety, a most flattering and exhilarating experience for a teacher.

THE STRAND PROJECT

To further engage the students in authentic research of their own heritage, to encourage creativity, and to meet the state curriculum requirement for oral presentation, I required a concluding project, with some details determined by which strand students had chosen. This project was the basis for the major unit grade; however, it also provided the greatest moments of shared compassion and emotion—key affective components in sustaining any community. The students had to create and present something they could pass on to their descendants, such as a videotape, a framed document, or an essay.

For the Romantic strand, the requirement was, Share with the class a story of a romantic nature that is directly associated with you or your family, such as how your parents or grandparents met or proposed or obstacles they had to overcome to be together. This assignment would, I felt, promote family conversation as the students engaged in meaningful research.

Hailey, who had been struggling academically in all subject areas, wrote a lengthy essay describing how her parents met and how her father knew immediately that he had met the woman he wished to spend his life with. The essay concluded with the fact that, 20 years later, he still felt that his first impression had been accurate. Hailey asked if I would read her paper aloud so she wouldn't "mess it up," and afterward students in the class were teary eyed and much more respectful of her than they had been before.

We were rolling with tears of laughter at another student's presentation. Frank had called his grandmother in California to ask how she and his grandfather had met, and he created a video using puppets to portray her story. Apparently Frank heard for the first time that she had at first preferred her husband's brother. The video included slapstick comedy with her yelling at him, "I don't know why I married you! I liked your brother best!" Frank won the admiration of our class for his creative screenplay, and the students asked to see the video again whenever we had time at the end of class.

The requirement for the Intergenerational strand was, Write the history of an object that has remained in your family for two or more generations, or prepare a document that can be passed on to your descendants. While I emphasized writing, I aimed for critical and creative thinking with this assignment, or for authentic research into an object, or, at best, for all three.

Michael, a previously quiet young man in our first-period class, brought a guitar for his Intergenerational presentation, saying that it was an object that wasn't very valuable in terms of money, but it had been passed down in his family. When his classmates asked him what he was going to play, he meekly responded, "You'll see." During his presentation, he told the class how his mother had taught him to play classical guitar, which she had learned from her father, and he was using a pick that had belonged to his grandfather. To the students' awe and admiration, Michael played one piece, and the class asked me if we could allow him to play more. I, too, was moved by his talent, and he said he would play one that we probably didn't know by guitarist Eric Clapton. He beautifully presented "Tears in Heaven," and some of us were soon in tears. Later that day, two students told me that Michael had been asked to play in the cafeteria during lunch. This was the first indication that the project assignment was affecting other aspects of school beyond my classroom.

Also in that class, Josh wrote a glowing tribute to his grandfather. He wished for his essay to be kept for his descendants, stating that the relationship of Chooj and his grandfather in *Mountain Windsong* reminded him of talks he had with his grandfather. He told of his grandfather's attending a ball game, even though his grandfather had to return to his job and work until 1:00 a.m. to meet a deadline. I was heartened to read in his reflection that, as a result of his reading, Josh had made a real connection with his grandfather that he will value in the years to come.

The most personal connections were presented through the Intergenerational strand by a student in the sixth-period class, the last class of the day, and the one that was the most ethnically diverse. Sherry, a troubled young mother who spent a great deal of her time in and out of in-school suspension, wrote a tribute to her mother in which she forgave her for her death 2 years previously from HIV. She then held up baby booties that her own son had worn as an infant and stated that she now realized that she was also leaving a legacy to her child, and she determined that it would be one of which he could be proud. Several listeners were in tears at this point, including me. Again the effects of the assignment were apparent outside the classroom: at a postplanning event, one of the in-school suspension supervisors commented that Sherry, previously one of his "regular attendees," hadn't received any discipline referrals the past few weeks of school.

ANALYSIS AND IMPLICATIONS

So many immeasurable learning experiences occurred during that novel unit. Students collaborated on the required assignments and completed their reading passages and worksheets and essays, but they also demonstrated respect and sensitivity for one another's artifacts and heritage. Of course, there were a few who neglected to bring an artifact for the initial presentation and hurriedly and obviously fictionalized a story of a dollar in imitation of my model. Perhaps I should have failed the impostors, but I found their imitations quite humorous and, following my lead, the class would also snicker, encouraging them to be even more hilarious in their defense. So we shared laughter, and the forgetful ones realized that one mistake did not cause total disaster. All students, however, took the final project presentation seriously, and although some were intentionally comical in tone, serious effort was evident in every piece.

Not only did the students treat one another with respect; I also felt that the teacher-student relationship was strengthened. Students would talk with me privately about the people they had written about. Even when Jenny, whose father had been imprisoned, was no longer in one of my classes, she came by to tell me that she had received a response to a letter she had written to him. Josh came by periodically to give me updates on his grandfather, who was ill for a time. Every student in those classes still speaks to me when we meet in the hallway.

I also made some personal connections during my own research for the unit. I contacted a cousin in Texas whom I hadn't heard from in 40 years, and he mailed me a packet of family history that he and my uncle had created as they visited sites in Texas to trace our Cherokee heritage through my great-grandmother. (My students found hilarious the story about my great-grandmother attempting to conceal a cow from Union troops.) I sent copies of the information and pictures to my own children, and one of my daughters is creating a family history for all our relatives. I am also in e-mail contact with that long-lost cousin.

We certainly created a friendly learning community, one that enabled students to risk rejection and scorn as we immersed ourselves in the story of the attempted degradation of a totally civilized nation of people, the Cherokee. The students comprehended the broken treaties, the misplaced trust, the heartbreak of separation, and the search for lost love that Conley relates in the novel. Beyond the novel, though, we researched our own heritage and realized our own legacies, and we experienced the diversity within our own classroom community. Hopefully, the students will continue to carry the acceptance and compassion we felt for one another and for the Cherokee Nation beyond the classroom, helping ensure that the

Paulding County of today, where newcomers and oldtimers have had trouble interacting, can develop a sense of unity and acceptance in the years ahead.

REFERENCES

Conley, R. (1992). *Mountain windsong.* Norman: University of Oklahoma Press.

Couch, J., & Marshall, B. (Producers/Directors). (1999). *The southeastern Indians* (Video). (Available from Georgia Department of Natural Resources, 2 Martin Luther King, Jr., Drive SE, Suite 1354, Atlanta, GA 30334)

Glancy, D. (1996). *Pushing the bear: A novel of the Trail of tears.* New York: Harcourt Brace.

Momaday, N. S. (1999). Extract from *The Way to Rainy Mountain.* In Dianne Cappillo, et al. (Eds.), *Literature: Timeless voices, timeless themes* (pp. 582–586). Upper Saddle River, NJ: Prentice Hall. (Original work published 1969)

CHAPTER 6

I Belong to This Place: Claiming a Neighborhood Landmark

Leslie Walker

"Times change . . . but I am confident that the earth itself will remain basically the same, continuing to shape the lives of its owners, for good or ill, as it has for millennia" (Carter, 2001, p. 271). I read those words from Jimmy Carter's memoir during the Keeping and Creating American Communities (KCAC) second summer institute in 2001, and they have stayed with me ever since. In fact, the idea of being shaped by a place has not only crept into my consciousness; it has moved into my classroom. It took a while, but the concept that who we are today is based on who was here before us has become a major component of my teaching philosophy. Where we've been does matter. Our lives are fashioned by where our families are from, what neighborhoods we live in, and where we call home. I look at places around me with a perspective that wasn't there before. And now I believe it is a perspective important for my students to have as well. I want them to take ownership in where they live, because, in part, it defines who they are.

During the first year of the KCAC project, I was a participant in the Recovering Displaced Heritages research team. Based on KCAC principles that through writing and collaboration we can research and recover a regional culture, we studied the Cherokee Removal and created texts (timeline, play, poetry) that could help keep that culture alive. Our theme team also became our own community of teacher-researchers studying the Removal together. Now when I cross the Chattahoochee River on my daily commute to school, from one Atlanta suburb to another, I think about the places on the river where the Cherokee lived. When I see certain county-line markers, I know the Cherokee once owned the land. The roadside market where I buy homegrown tomatoes was once an Indian trading post, and the spot where the real estate office stands was once a Cherokee Removal site. Having been immersed in gathering knowledge of the Cherokee, I began to value their culture and appreciate how they contributed to my community. That knowledge matters because it gives me ownership in "this place."

My commute to school is 30 minutes, one way. I go through the same traffic lights, sit behind the same school buses on the road, and pass the same landmarks, 5 days a week. My mind is usually busy with lesson plans, phone calls, and committee meetings. Before I know it, I'm in the high school parking lot and ready for the day to begin. Until I joined the KCAC project, I didn't really pay much attention to the world outside my car.

But one morning, in the year after our second summer institute, while waiting for the light to turn green, I mused on a sign stretched across the wrought-iron gates of a roadside cemetery: "Volunteers Needed Smyrna Cemetery Association." Beyond the rails of the gate lay Smyrna's Historical Cemetery in great disrepair: overgrown grasses and bushes, a flower vase on its side, and tree branches on top of grave markers. And although I had seen that same sign and cemetery for several years, on this day it struck me as ironic. Because on this day, a big, fat, yellow John Deere bulldozer was cozily idling, about one foot away from that "hallowed" site. Construction had begun on phase 2 of the city of Smyrna's award-winning complex, complete with town homes, offices, and retail space. The light turned green and I drove on to school. But something had clicked in my brain.

I walked into school that morning with a plan forming in my mind. Could I take the transient and diverse community of my classroom and transform it into a group of collaborators who care about the place where they live? Could I invite them to "recover" something that was being displaced and have that recovery process become a natural part of their consciousness—a perspective—that could be used in other parts of their lives? Could my students use research and writing to recover the stories in that cemetery? Could they reflect on the impact that new construction would have on their neighborhood? Would the process make it matter for them? Would they take ownership and claim this place? Would they care? What role could writing play in this culture-making process?

THE SCHOOL COMMUNITY

I teach 10th-grade Literature and Composition to regular education students at Campbell High School in Smyrna, Georgia. The population of

Smyrna, considered part of metropolitan Atlanta, has grown and changed. A population of 255 in 1880 grew to one of 19,157 in 1970, when only two people were documented as "non-White" (Harold Smith, personal interview, 29 June, 2002). Today's population stands at 45,000 and is diverse in a number of ways. The high school has grown and changed as well. Today, Campbell's enrollment totals 2,040 students, representing 26 nationalities and the largest Hispanic enrollment in the county. Campbell's population includes 5% Asian, 43% African American, 14% Hispanic, 35% Caucasian, and 2% multiracial ("Student Enrollment," 2002). In any given semester, withdrawal and enrollment numbers can reach up to 200 students. One of my 10th-grade classes has a combination of 15 regular ed students and Wendy Walker's six special ed students, and class members call places like Detroit, Chicago, New York, St. Louis, Mexico, and Haiti "home." Only 2 out of the 21 who participated in the project described here can make the claim of being native to Smyrna. Home is someplace else for them.

THE PLAN

During the first school year (2000–2001) of the KCAC project, one of the assigned texts for our teacher study group was *My Place*, a picture book by Nadia Wheatley and Donna Rawlins (1994). The Australian writer presents the history of the Botany Bay region of Australia through the voices and drawings of fictional children. The one constant in the text is a fig tree that stands the test of time as 200 years pass by. Landmarks change, people change, customs change, but the tree remains. The book jacket sums up Wheatley's message: "Everyone is a part of history, and every place has a story as old as the earth." Each young voice begins his or her story with "This is my place," yet the final voice makes a powerful change to this assertion, claiming instead that "I belong to this place" (Wheatley, 1994, n.p.). Thus, I began the semester by reading this book with my classes.

Based on the philosophy that the classroom is a community in itself, and valuing the places that each student comes from, this activity helped build and foster a sense of community in our mutual place. Just as Wheatley explores the layers of history in Botany Bay, I wanted my students to explore the layers of history in Smyrna. A trip to the cemetery would be the catalyst for meeting my instructional goal: conducting authentic research to produce written text.

I shared my ideas about a field trip with Wendy: If we want our students to take ownership in where they live, why don't we take a walking field trip to Smyrna's museum and cemetery? On the way back, we can stop for lunch at the new Smyrna Deli. It's all only one mile from the school, and these kids ride everywhere. Do they ever take the time to walk and take notice of what's around them? Let's make it two trips— the first to become familiar with the two sites, and the second to clean up the cemetery. My rationale was that the first trip would instill a sense of community ownership in our students, which would naturally result in a burning desire for a second trip to make the cemetery respectable. Maybe I could elicit a consciousness of the juxtaposition of the old and the new Smyrna. The outcome of all this would be a writing component designed to demonstrate the students' sense of Old Smyrna. Wendy and I brainstormed possible products: a personal narrative created from a name on a tombstone, a historical account of Smyrna in the 1800s, a poem about the changes taking place, a journal from the point of view of a teenager in the 1800s, a timeline of the city, or a play about the neighborhood.

I completed a field trip request form. When I came to the section about how this trip relates to the curriculum, I felt confident in my response: "Working collaboratively, students will conduct authentic research with primary sources (museum and cemetery) to produce written text showing their understanding of their place in the community." Not only would this trip easily meet the writing and research expectations of the 10th-grade literature curriculum (composition to include creative, expressive, and personal writing; research activities to include personal history and interview); it would also incorporate several key principles of KCAC-based teaching: retaining regional cultures, writing to create community, forming community cultures, and researching community texts. While I waited for approval, the weeks went by, and I went to work on what I thought would be the biggest challenge of this plan—engaging the class.

One day after school, I stopped by the Smyrna Deli & Ice Cream, located in the Village Pavilion of Smyrna's new city complex. I introduced myself to the owner and shared my plan with her. She was thrilled with the idea and said that for 5 dollars each she could provide box lunches for my students, as long as I let her know one day in advance. As I drove home that afternoon, my mind worked as I envisioned my students having fun with lunch after the tour. But my ulterior motive was for them to make a connection between the value of the old (the cemetery next to the city complex—*retaining regional cultures*) and the value of the new (the deli—*forming community cultures*). Most of the students have never been in the deli or taken advantage of the amenities provided in the complex. I wanted it to become *their* museum, *their* cemetery, and *their* deli.

ENGAGING THE STUDENTS

Although I knew the students would be responsive to the idea of any kind of field trip, I wasn't sure they would like what I had in mind. And although I had introduced the idea of this trip casually to the class before, saying we would go one day in the spring on a walking field trip, during which we would clean up the cemetery and have lunch, I thought with writing I could get some genuine feedback about the plan. So one day I wrote the following prompt on the board: "We're planning a trip to Smyrna's museum and cemetery. Do you see any value in this trip? Please be honest and reflect on any pros or cons. Why should we go?"

Alicia yelled out that she was not cleaning up some old cemetery that was nasty. But the written responses were more encouraging. Not only were they honest; they were reassuring. My students were interested in the trip for varying reasons: they were new to Smyrna; they wanted some hands-on experience; they had never been to a cemetery; they liked the idea of visiting a local museum; they were looking forward to having the class go on a trip—even a short one to a nearby site—together. Several of the written reflections expressed interest in exploring "the story" behind the cemetery.

"Yes," I thought as I read these, "there is some kind of story behind it. And yes, maybe we can learn about something that can help us later on in life." I was encouraged by their responses. They were already engaged in two KCAC principles: inquiring about and critiquing a community text. I saw them accepting my invitation to "recover" something that was being displaced and to have that recovery process become a perspective that could be used in other parts of their lives.

THE TRIP

The semester moved on as we covered the curriculum and waited for that spring day that would allow the opportunity for a break from the traditional classroom setting. We had permission slips signed, and I collected lunch money from each student. I purchased two throwaway cameras for the students to document the trip and we were off.

The morning was wet and humid, but a clearing sky promised better weather to come. We took the sidewalk from the school through the older neighborhood that sits next to the city complex, forming small, casual talking groups as we went. Jokes were made about a dilapidated house, windows boarded up and yard overgrown. "Moving in, Ms. Walker?" Several houses were for sale; several had that newly remodeled look, with vinyl siding and swept front yards. We wondered at the garbage cans, buried at the front curb of each yard. One simply had to lift a hinged lid to drop trash into the receptacle. From the front stoop of a house with a "For Rent" sign in a window, an unchained dog barked menacingly.

"We'll protect you, Ms. Walker!" the class chimed. The community formed in my classroom was becoming the one I had visualized earlier in the year, the one claiming its place in the neighborhood and caring about it. And we were forming our own new community culture as we went. Paul, quiet and aloof in class, took the lead as we walked down the sidewalk. We all followed behind, in pairs or in threes. Tawn and Ashley, who never talk to each other in class, were walking together, making a new friendship.

"Watch out!" Andy yelled protectively to Kelvin, who was walking down the middle of the street. "There's a car coming!" Josh and Ian made jokes. Chris pulled at Leslie's hair. Matt took pictures and dragged his feet at the back of the group.

The sun was out in full force by the time we arrived at the museum. I stepped inside to warn the curators we had arrived while Wendy gathered the class for a group picture in front of the building. Wendy also distributed a handout with the following directions: list five facts you learned from the museum; pick one of the historical markers in the cemetery and copy the information from the marker; write five questions you have from your experience today; what would you like to know more about? The guided writing on-site would serve as an instrument to collect data and as a question-generating exercise that could be used later for research and reflection.

My students signed the guestbook, and some commented that they were beginning to learn more about Smyrna's history. They posed for pictures next to a mannequin dressed in an old Campbell High band uniform. They rang the domed bell and pored over display cases of World War II memorabilia. They gazed at photographs showing how Smyrna had changed over the past 100 years. They collaborated to gather information for their worksheets, and after thanking the curators for their help, we stepped next door to Aunt Fanny's Cabin.

Aunt Fanny's Cabin now serves as Smyrna's welcome center, but for 5 decades it had been a popular restaurant, known throughout the country as a "favorite southern-themed dining spot." The walls are lined with autographed photos of both movie stars and sports celebrities who visited the restaurant. A museum volunteer gathered the class around her and read information about the cabin from a pamphlet.

Because I am a native of Atlanta, I know some of the history of the restaurant. I know that it is restored plantation slave quarters, and I know

that Aunt Fanny was African American. And although her picture is displayed proudly in the restaurant, no mention is made of the fact that she
was the cook, not the owner. I watched my students as they listened attentively to the volunteer, but I could see questions in their eyes as they
tried to understand the story they were hearing. They were hungry for
more information. Shuffling their feet and nudging each other, they appeared doubtful or unsatisfied. They could sense an absence of information and they were trying to figure it out on their own. The inquiry process
had started—they had just been invited to recover something that was
being displaced.

From Aunt Fanny's Cabin, we stepped across the street to Smyrna's
Memorial Cemetery. Some students were superstitious and refused to step
off the memorial bricks that ran from the entrance to the middle of the
cemetery, but others roamed freely. Wendy and two students deep in conversation walked to the far end of the cemetery. One student snapped
pictures furiously, capturing the graves against the unavoidable backdrop
of construction. I watched another student as he leaned against the
wrought-iron fence at the back of the cemetery and stared at the construction several feet away. Concrete trucks were pouring and hammers were
pounding.

"Look, here's a new grave, Ms. Walker," someone called out.

"Why are there so many unknown markers?" they all asked.

"It's so sad."

Their writing assignment on this part of the trip was to copy down
information from one of the several historical markers on the site. They
also had to write five questions about something they wanted to know
more about. They were fascinated by the fact that there were so many
unidentified markers. As they had done at the museum, they were notic-
ing the absence of presence.

By now we had been on the road for more than an hour and a half.
One by one the students gathered along the stone wall that marked the
cemetery's boundary. Lunch was foremost on everyone's mind, so after a
group photo along the cemetery's curb, we headed for the deli.

Although I had envisioned picking up our box lunches, then eating
outside around the square's water fountain (this is where I wanted them
to have the old-and-new-can-live-together moment, as well as a great
photo shot), the class had other plans.

"It's too hot out there, Ms. Walker."

So we ate inside, in an air-conditioned common area adjacent to the
deli, where the class could easily get refills on drinks, order another sand-
wich, or buy an ice cream cone. The tall round tables and stools welcomed
us, and classmates sat with new and old friends alike. Then with one last

drink refill and the screeching of high chairs on the wood floor, we reluctantly headed back to school.

But along the way, we stopped at the center of the village green to sit around the fountain, finish ice cream cones, and take several group photos. A less direct route home took us by the pond that borders the city complex. Ducks were chased, sticks were dragged, and rocks were thrown into the water, as we lazily made our way back to school. I felt as though I was on a family vacation, driving somewhere, when after lunch everyone wants to fall asleep in the back of the van.

ARTIFACTS PRODUCED

Before my students left class that day, they turned in the cameras so I could get the film developed, and they turned in the five questions generated from Wendy's handout. These included the following:

- Why are there so many unknown people in the cemetery?
- Where does Aunt Fanny's family reside? Do they still stay in Smyrna?
- Why was the house of Aunt Fanny so popular to the people?
- How come there [aren't] many African Americans in the museum?
- How did she claim ownership as a Black in those days?

I include these questions because they show the inquiry process my students were going through. They were asking some of the same questions I had asked months ago as I sat at that traffic light. And they have begun to answer those questions. They *are* collaborators who care about the place where they live. They *are* starting to "recover" something that is being displaced. They *are* starting to show an understanding of their place in the community. They do care.

Once the pictures from our field trip were developed, I thought creating storyboards would provide closure and assessment of understanding. I had the class, in self-selected groups of four, arrange the pictures, which I divided randomly among them, in any way they wanted to create a storyboard about our trip. The storyboards took on different personalities, not necessarily displayed in "order of event" format, but each telling a story just the same. One group focused on the names of the deceased in the cemetery. Another group focused on the time spent at lunch, "chillin in the deli," then "talking and sitting in the shade." A third group wrote about being impressed by "the fact that," at the Smyrna cemetery, "the old and the new combine to form one place."

ANALYSIS AND IMPLICATIONS

A month later, I drove to the Smyrna Museum. I was in the throes of writing this essay and searching for statistics on the city of Smyrna. It was a summer Saturday and traffic wasn't too bad. On the corner before the city square, a baseball team was having a fund-raising fish fry. The "Volunteers Needed" sign still stretched across the wrought-iron gates of the Smyrna Memorial Cemetery. Where once the John Deere bulldozer dozed, an almost completed mixed-use complex included 18 townhouses built above retail stores and restaurants.

I thought about the project I had done with my students and wondered if, how, and when I would implement it again. Of course, I would! And I won't wait until the end of a semester. Imagine the products that would be generated if we began this type of inquiry at the beginning of the semester and folded it into the regular curriculum. What better way to study place than in Contemporary Lit, which emphasizes world cultures, exemplified by the students in my classroom.

It's really quite simple, such a little thing. We just walk down the street to the local museum and cemetery. No buses to order, no searching for chaperones, no overnight permission slips. We talk to one another, we write with one another, and we discover things about one another and our community that we have never known before nor would ever find out. Ultimately, we realize that we belong to this place. And I find beauty in that simplicity. As clichéd as it may sound, learning can take place in our own backyards. We all have that place in our neighborhood that can be a catalyst for our students to research and recover; write about and reflect on. It can start small and grow big, or just stay small. It doesn't matter. What *does* matter is the ownership our students take in where they live, something that will stay with them the rest of their lives.

REFERENCES

Carter, J. (2001). *An hour before daylight*. New York: Simon and Schuster.
Student enrollment. In *Information technology: Georgia Department of Education*. Retrieved September 7, 2002 from http://techservices.doe.k12.ga.us/admin/reports/studentinfo.htm
Wheatley, N., & Rawlins, D. (1994). *My place*. New York: Kane/Miller.

CHAPTER 7

Composing Communities: College Students Become Real Research Writers

Linda Stewart

In the early days of every semester, students sometimes employ the phrase "real life" to mean a state existing outside the classroom. They assume that their classroom experiences are somehow isolated from real-life activities and that they are, in fact, just treading water. This assumption is a bit deflating to educators across the United States who, like myself, opt for the teaching life in a classroom venue. Aren't students and teachers living real life in a classroom as they write cogent arguments, apply a scientific method, design a business model, or read a historic document? While teachers may share this belief, it is not always easy to convince students that classroom experiences are indeed connected to real life.

Students' perceptions of our classroom changed once the local landscape of metro Atlanta became the focus for our university composition course, which emphasizes interdisciplinary research and writing. This change resulted from my collaboration with the team investigating the suburban strand "Shifting Landscapes, Converging Peoples" during the 2000 summer institute for Keeping and Creating American Communities (KCAC). I began asking students to locate evidence of communities in our surrounding region. This emphasis on regional research within the arc of community studies deepened our inquiry into the history, politics, economics, and social values of our surroundings. Eventually, students not only realized the complex connections between the classroom and their region, but also discovered much about themselves and their own assumptions as they wrote about and discussed their findings. While this approach yielded many surprises and benefits, the confluence of classroom and community was the most dramatic change.

I didn't anticipate how well this inductive approach to research would work, but I was confident that the conceptual base provided by KCAC was sound. Readings from Kenneth Jackson's (1985) *Crabgrass Frontier: The Suburbanization of the United States*, Dolores Hayden's (1999) *Power of Place: Urban Landscapes as Public History*, Joel Garreau's (1992) *Edge City: Life on the New Frontier*, and Benedict Anderson's (1981) *Imagined Communities: Reflections on the Origin and Spread of Nationalism* provided specific and spatial concepts for beginning an investigation into our region. These texts—as well as memoirs, ethnographies, and novels—illustrated how the concepts of community, landscape, space, and place are conceived differently in various disciplines. Thus, examining our region provided opportunities for the students to unravel the competing and often cooperative forces that shaped communities of the past. This understanding then helped them to understand the present complexities in their physical and personal lives.

The general education classes I teach and the student groups involved are especially well suited to this effort. In particular, the second required course in the English composition sequence at Kennesaw State University focuses on interdisciplinary research and writing. Although everyone in the class in any given term would have already had one college writing course, there would still be a wide range in ability, past academic work, and life experience. (Kennesaw State, now a regional university with graduate programs and an enrollment approaching 19,000, continues to serve a substantial number of older, part-time, commuter students alongside 18-year-olds who are living in the campus's new dorms.) Facing such a diverse pool of students while trying to teach some basic research and writing skills, I have found through my work in the KCAC program that framing the course around community studies can provide rigorous yet engaging learning experiences that capitalize on students' shared interest in where they live.

REAL RESEARCH

Hayden (1999) calls community research "cultural landscape studies." She explains this framework as a way of reading and understanding history from a broadly defined physical environment that might include the city, its structures, or its inhabitants (p. 19). She asserts that cultural landscape studies should be "grounded in both the aesthetics of experiencing places with all five senses and the politics of experiencing places as contested territory" (p. 43). This assertion validated my students' efforts to experience their region and eventually understand the political implications of their work. Lucy Lippard (1997), in her book *The Lure of the Local*, complicates landscape studies and provides many angles from which to study one's region. She explains that landscape may be viewed as "a complex social construction or produced space" with "records of hybrid culture, hybrid histories that must be woven into a new mainstream" (pp. 8–9). Additionally, the Western writer Mary Austin (1987) reminds us in editor Melody Graulich's *Western Trails: A Collection of Short Stories* that "to understand the fashion of any life, one must know the land it is lived in and the procession of the year" (p. 31). Therefore, for my students to make sense of their lives and future choices, they needed to know their region and how it evolved over time.

Consequently, students in my class researched a once rural, now suburban frontier in metro Atlanta by examining the artifacts, buildings, images, and natural spaces of suburbia. Jackson (1985), in his seminal work, *Crabgrass Frontier*, suggests "that the space around us—the physical organization of neighborhoods, roads, yards, houses, and apartments—sets up living patterns that condition our behavior" (p. 3). When students examine the "spaces around them," they begin to see the connections between the personal and the public. They discover connections between the individual and her or his social and physical environment. They experience the politics of space by examining it firsthand. They may not know what they are seeing initially. But that's partly what teachers are for—to tease their thinking and to provide context.

To help students begin this inquiry, I first asked them to find evidence of communities, including T-shirts, museum exhibitions, homeless shelters, garage sales, yard art, local parades, war memorials, and bulletin boards. Hayden (1999) invites her readers to examine the "complex forces that led to the present configuration" (p. 42). This phrase was particularly useful in my class because my charge is to introduce students to writing across the disciplines. If they must untangle the forces (from many "disciplines") that appear in the "configurations" of their local landscape, they begin to understand not only the history of that structure, but also the social web woven into it. To further our inquiry, we discussed our local environment, viewed photographs and films, read local newspapers, and generated lists of communities in our region. These lists provided ample evidence of the rich spectrum of community life, and from these brainstorming sessions, students honed their interests and developed initial questions.

Probably the most important questions were, "What isn't there?" and "Why not?" These two questions actually politicize our research. To research what presently exists is to take a limited view. To ask what isn't there is to seek and uncover the voices of our culture that have been ignored or suppressed. Prepared by brainstorming sessions and discussions about the nature of communities, students began to investigate their region through primary research activities.

PRIMARY RESEARCH

In *The Curious Researcher*, Bruce Ballenger (2001) explains that students are seldom active researchers. He aptly points out that student research writers often "assume that the academic writer always sets out to *prove* rather than *to find out*, that she scrupulously avoids ambiguity and is more concerned with answers than questions" (p. xxiii). I agree. If students begin with a topic and "working thesis," searching secondary sources to find others to support their point of view, they are not necessarily real researchers engaged in creating meaning. Georgia Rhoades and Lynn Moss Sanders (2001) assert in "Creating Knowledge Through Primary Research" that "primary research allows the student writer to choose topics of real interest and to become a real authority, presenting research and results to readers who cannot know the subject as well" (p. 70). Like Ballenger, they emphasize the shift in authority from the teacher to the student.

While I agree that action and authority are close companions, I'd like to suggest even further that the topic should not precede the research activity. Before I joined the KCAC community of teacher researchers, typically I had encouraged students to find a topic they were curious about or one they felt strongly about exploring. We spent considerable time brainstorming topic ideas. Students then found scholarly sources in several disciplines and eventually determined an angle and a controlling idea that they could develop fully. While this is a valid approach, I now emphasize the intuitive and inductive nature of primary research, which creates a bit of frustration for some students. While many are curious and willing, others don't like not knowing what their thesis is before they begin. I spend quite a bit of time reassuring them and providing examples from former classes. As a result, their research has become more trenchant and ambitious.

Over the past 3 years, students have researched franchise coffeehouses, corporate clothing meccas, and suburban real estate developments. Quirkier places are the prescription or hygiene counters of a grocery store and the magazine stand at Borders Bookstore or the entrance to Wal-Mart. They have investigated the history of a rock barn, the Silver Comet rail trail (a hiking/biking path), and the Kennesaw Mountain Civil War Battlefield. They have observed classrooms and pool halls, homeless shelters and town squares, playgrounds and traffic intersections. They have interviewed a hotel chain CEO, a nursing home resident, a war veteran, a prison inmate, members of a gay and lesbian organization on campus, a grandparent, a chemistry professor, a pediatric dentist, an immigrant to the Untied States, a family caretaker, an interracial couple, a Pentecostal minister, and a 6-year-old beauty pageant contestant. Their research into the sights and stories of their region emerges from assignments that emphasize site observations and interviews as primary research activities.

SITE OBSERVATION

A site observation is an effective research activity for students early in the semester because they can take a less prominent role than in an interview. This type of research can be pragmatic—whether the activity is selecting a college, scouting a sports team, locating a home site, choosing a day care or assisted-living facility, or finding a fishable lake. Beyond practicality, however, site observations create opportunities for students to become more critical thinkers. One student commented, "When I took on the role of observer, I noticed the things I had neglected to see, and I stopped to think about other things that go unnoticed."

Asking students to conduct a site observation often elicits puzzled looks. Providing examples and a rationale helps the students understand the process. Rhoades's and Sanders' (2001) "Creating Knowledge Through Primary Research," in *The Subject is Research*, and Chiseri-Strater's and Sunstein's (1997) "Researching Place: The Spatial Gaze," in *FieldWorking: Reading and Writing Research*, are excellent resources. After several terms of teaching composition with a community focus, I am now able to cite the places my former students have visited and how they ultimately developed their papers.

Once students become engaged in this first research assignment, they often conduct what I think of as street talks. At the students' chosen site, they ask people, informally, what the latter's viewpoints are. At the historic Marietta Town Square, George stopped several town residents—park goers, children, businesspeople at lunch, store owners, and a homeless person. He talked to all of them about their impressions of the town square. He knew it as a child and he wanted to understand this place in its current usage. His essay, titled "My Marietta Square," with an emphasis on "My," revealed his nostalgia for the past—for the public square and for his own childhood. Like George, many students are talking to community members whose comments are finding their way into the students' essays. Somewhat surprisingly, no one has reported a negative experience. They are talking to people in malls, parks, restaurants, county buildings, nursing homes, and more. These informal discussions give them the courage to build up to the Interview assignment—"Conversations on Community Culture."

Later in the semester the students identify someone they want to interview. Some use the formal interview as an opportunity to explore a career choice, but many choose a community leader. The assignment requires that the students investigate a community that they do *not* presently participate in, so as to initiate conversations across community boundaries. Students often discover that their assumptions about a particular community that they have avoided or might wish to join are somewhat shaky. The students are understandably nervous, but again, we take time developing good questions and practicing interviewing techniques in class. Chapter 5 in *The Bedford Guide to the Research Process, 2nd edition* (Johnson, 1992) and Chapter 7 in *The Subject Is Research* (Bishop & Zemliansky, 2001) are two good resources, offering helpful information and tips for conducting an interview. My students' interview stories also provide the substance for our class discussions. Perhaps it's my ongoing discomfort with a teacher-driven agenda, but I believe in letting the students' stories shape the classroom discourse. I trust that their work will carry us into topics of consequence. Thus, it becomes apparent during class discussions that their personal research topics have very public implications.

Students often conduct powerful interviews that affect the classroom community. David, a young White man, had shown an interest all semester in issues involving race and decided he wanted to interview an interracial couple. An African American woman in our class, Carol, offered to let him interview her and her White husband. Having been married for several years and raising two children, she and her husband were very willing to talk to David about the opportunities and challenges they had faced.

David presented his paper in class, freeing the audience to discuss race without a teacher-led agenda. One anecdote Carol told involved her husband's visit to her church—an all African American Southern Baptist Church. He was the only White man. She described his discomfort with the service. Hearing about this experience led my class to an honest, probing discussion about familiarity with certain rituals—religious and secular, cultural and racial. What struck me at the time was how the class addressed in depth what might be considered "hot" topics in a way that precluded rancor as they showed curiosity and empathy for one another. Certainly I participated in the class discussion and summarized some of the key points they made. I'm not advocating a complete hands-off approach. But I've found the students to be far more open minded and thoughtful about issues once they have interviewed an individual within a certain community, so they are the ones introducing the topics into the classroom. Research into one's region will always promote discussions of race and gender, class and ethnicity, if it is conducted thoughtfully and carefully. In addition, the personal connection made during an interview helps to break down misconceptions and false assumptions.

Another student, Linda, decided she wanted to break free from what she perceived to be her secluded suburban life. She wanted to better understand communities she did not come in contact with in her daily life. She wanted to find an ignored community, one with little power or voice. She was also interested in children's issues. So she arranged for an interview with a local prison inmate to better understand what happened to children when their mothers were incarcerated. To secure that interview, she was very tenacious. In her reflection about the interview she wrote, "In light of this experience, I completed this paper with an entirely different perspective on the cycle of poverty and its devastating repercussions. I could work on a project like this for months or years and still uncover new ideas; I certainly hope that my future studies will offer the opportunity to do just that!" Her research piqued everyone's interest, and every day as she came to class, a student would ask her about the progress of her findings. We were all surprised to hear how many women were incarcerated for what Linda called "crimes of poverty." The woman she interviewed had written a bad check and stolen some money. She had been sentenced to several years in prison and her mother was taking care of her children. Linda discovered an outreach program for women in prison and was considering becoming a volunteer. The last paragraph of her researched essay, describing the woman she interviewed, reveals the power of her experience:

> One of [this inmate's] most poignant comments occurred when she talked about starting every new day. Each morning, as her mind slowly focuses back into wakefulness, she opens her eyes, looks around the cell, and thinks to herself, "Oh my God, I'm in prison." I had experienced that same thought while I waited for her in the interview room; maybe we are not as different as I thought we were.

While Linda made a personal connection through a public interview, others discovered the public within the personal. Students who choose to interview friends or family members often uncover an aspect of that individual's history that they previously didn't know existed. Thus, a student might interview a grandparent, seemingly well known to her or him. Lee Ann interviewed her grandmother about the latter's experience as a

Russian exile. Mary interviewed her father, who was a child of the Great Depression. They began to see that individual in the context of public experience, whether as a war veteran, an immigrant, or a religious convert. The students, as primary researchers, realized that people they know have lived lives of significance.

From these two primary research activities, students have become more wary consumers as they rediscover the logo-laden landscape they live in. They have learned the history of their region. They have begun to understand the forces shaping the communities that surround them. They listened to family stories and immigrant exile narratives; they examined political and civic issues as participant/observers of their region; and they began to carve out their positions within or outside these communities as they wrote their reports and essays. Examining the structures of their cultural landscape through site observations and listening to community participants through interviews both empower students and galvanize the classroom. The act of writing about their research certainly creates meaning for the students, but often their work resonates well beyond our classroom community.

PUBLIC WRITING

If, as Jackson (1985) claims, a good essay is a "product of experience joined to scholarly thought," then students must join their findings and analysis of their primary research to a larger body of work (p. 10). Adapting this KCAC-consistent principle, after my students have conducted their research, they begin reading academic articles that connect to their subject matter. Encouraging them to read journal articles across disciplines underscores the multifaceted nature of their research and validates their work. Betty, a student researching the Silver Comet Trail, an old railroad transformed into a nature trail that will eventually connect Atlanta to the state of Alabama, found the scores of federal, state, and municipal laws that were passed to create what is commonly called a "rail trail." She read sociological and psychological studies that explained the benefits of family bonding through outdoor activities. She read about nature preservation, the lack of exercise in suburban environments, and the railroad industry. Ultimately, she decided that what most interested her was the legislation and cooperation necessary to transform this former railroad line into its present incarnation as a community nature trail. She focused her paper on that aspect. Her experience of visiting the trail, accessing the Web site, and reading local newspaper stories was combined with examining government and scholarly sources. Her essay was a combination of experience and scholarly thought.

Powerful writing also emerges when students have a real audience—the public. When I first began to adapt KCAC strategies for my teaching, I was unaware of the impossibility of keeping our writing within the classroom. I thought our essays would be shared among ourselves, or occasionally sent out for publication. But the students' ideas and their research immediately demanded and created some unexpected audiences.

One student asked if she might observe her hometown of 300 residents in one of our region's still-rural areas. She wasn't sure how to begin, but she said there were only four structures in the town: the convenience store/post office, a working dairy farm, a Baptist church, and a sports field. Her first paper included photos of these structures and some analysis of the purposes of these places in her community. In the course of writing her essay, this student had talked to several of the townspeople, informally asking questions and gathering some amusing anecdotes about the town. The day her paper was due, she rushed in late, apologizing and explaining that she was delayed because she had had several phone calls before she left. A number of town residents and her pastor had called to wish her well on her paper for her English class.

This student decided to stay with her topic to revise and develop another essay. She decided that, rather than using the buildings to structure her narrative, she wanted stories from the residents. The post office donated the stamps for 300 letters with the same opening question: "Why is it important to remember what happened in our community's history and why is it important to preserve the way of life found here . . . ?" Over the following few weeks, two or three letters appeared in her mailbox every day. Residents began to arrive at her back door to be sure that she had their stories, with the hope that they would appear in her paper. She received love stories, poems, and letters. Because my student chose to ask and to listen to her neighbors' stories, she became the town historian. At the end of the semester, she said that gathering this information might provide a lifelong interest for her. She initiated the important work of creating and preserving that town's history, expanding her research, and writing from the classroom to her town community.

THE NECESSITY FOR REFLECTION

In addition to appreciating the importance of real audiences, it's necessary to realize that primary researchers need ample time to gather their material and reflect upon what they have gathered before they can write a cogent, polished essay. The writing-process or portfolio-based classroom provides for revision and time to write. However, I've found that the initial writing requirements need to be adapted to fit the curriculum. Rhoades and Sanders (2001) offer a report model in their essay that provides a template for writing up primary research. They note how the teacher's role changes as "we read the results of primary research" and how important it is to become "readers trying to follow the work of the paper to determine its clarity" (p. 70). To accommodate the roughness of the student's initial work, I have used a report model adapted from Dr. Sarah Robbins's honors seminar that organizes the writing around three parts: a report, a reflection, and an analysis. This initial report dovetails with the purpose of the site observation or interview, offering students time and space in which to gather their thoughts and begin to identify a focus. One goal should be to help writers key into an aspect of their research that they could then develop further through secondary sources. This initial report can then be revised into an argument with a controlling idea. Helping students elicit their emerging thesis is the most delicate act, because the students' research is so wide in scope and one does not want to quash their particular angle of inquiry.

I like to think that my students are writing what Zagarell (1988) calls "narratives of community" or what Hayden (1999) might describe as social history essays. As students uncover and come to understand the nature of communities and the history of their region, their writing contributes to and shapes the social landscape, creating meaning for themselves and others.

GETTING REAL

The activist nature of the KCAC approach has created some spontaneous combustion in my classroom. How often does a teacher have a group of students ask if they can work together to create a proposal to the university? Most academic writing stays within the classroom. In my experience, students don't seek extra work that isn't assigned. But they did in the fall semester of 2001. A team of research writers were organized in my classroom after September 11. Because my students were just beginning site-observation reports, several decided in the course of one class discussion that they wanted to conduct their research in New York City. Eight students worked for 2 weeks, meeting during and outside class hours to create a proposal that included biographies, an action plan, fund-raising ideas, and a letter to the president of the university. Their proposal, developed with great enthusiasm and genuine concern, was to visit the site of 9/11 and record in text and images what they observed. Their intent was to present their information to provide a forum for university students. The writing that emerged from their work was more than 20 pages, which, considering the length of a typical writing assignment, was extensive. Each student contributed to parts of the proposal, and they all collaborated to type, edit, and proofread the drafts and the finals. I met with them outside class to provide help when they wanted it, but mostly I watched them brainstorm, problem-solve, imagine their audience, determine their purpose, and write careful, thoughtful prose. Unfortunately, their proposal wasn't accepted. Interestingly, one of the reasons was that this spontaneous group wasn't under the auspices of an existing university student organization. No one knew quite what to do with this student group. Although understandably disappointed, they were proud of the effective way they worked together to deliver a professional proposal.

Consider the research they conducted: contacting universities in New York for possible housing, calling airlines for lowest fares, networking with friends, exploring fund-raising sources, reading newspapers and campus publications, and much more. Seeing them at work and reading their final proposal made for two of the most powerful and privileged moments in my teaching career. I only wish I had videotaped their workshop meetings to share with other teachers the genuine nature of their collaboration and careful consideration of their final product. But beyond all the work that they did, these students were very brave. They were willing to travel when it was considered very dangerous. Their parents wouldn't let them go unless I accompanied them. We agreed that if our proposal were accepted, we would all make the trip. Frankly, I'm a nervous traveler in the best of circumstances, but the students' earnest desire to create meaning out of that horrible event for our student population would have propelled me onto that plane. No matter what the outcome, it was clear to all the students that their writing was meaningful and powerful, because they had identified real audiences. They wrote with personal purpose and evoked a public response.

ANALYSIS AND IMPLICATIONS

As a result of the KCAC approach to community life and research, I have found that my students and I are talking and writing more about religion, race, class, and gender in more authentic ways. We examine current academic conversations about how to include faith-based expression (Rand, 2001, p. 356); how to make "whiteness visible" (Marshall & Ryden, 2000, p. 242); how to include gay, lesbian, and bisexual perspectives, not as a controversial issue, but "as a way of loving and living" (Hart, 1996, p. 121); and how to think about constructions of class, and all these topics are addressed through this curriculum. This approach nudges the teacher from the subject position to a place working alongside students as they research and write about communities. Thus, this curriculum avoids the "limitations of the pedagogy of white teachers who teach texts by 'minority' authors to address multiculturalism" (Marshall & Ryden, 2000, p. 242). The landscape is another text, and we read what it is and what we think it should become. We study theory and texts by authors of various racial, cultural, ethnic, economic, and religious backgrounds. But we read them *in addition to* reading our surroundings. Thus, work will emerge, such as Leslie's examination of her stepfather's conversion from Mormonism, Matthew's essay about the status of gay and lesbian organizations on campus, and Ashley's exploration of a beauty contest for toddlers. And sharing stories about this research as it was in progress has initiated class discussions about religion, sexuality, gender, and children's rights.

Robert Putnam (2000), in *Bowling Alone*, describes the importance of investigating communities and experiencing research. Like Putnam, Hayden (1999) underscores the importance of experiential research into community as a significant element in social change. I didn't become a teacher to change the world. I wanted to teach to share a love of reading and writing with my students and to help them discover themselves and the world through literature and writing. But as I have adapted the KCAC practices described here, my role has changed, because my students' work has changed. No longer merely student centered—which still implies the teacher's agenda—the classroom has become community centered. The students' experiences, to date, have generated connections among families, town residents, campus groups, historical societies, federal prisons, fund-raising groups, and neighborhoods.

Although I've always taught with the intent to create community within my classroom, I must become the teacher that activist students require. Thus, I need to be aware of finding audiences for my students, anticipating their needs as they move into community work, and providing networking opportunities for them to showcase their work beyond the classroom. Don Mitchell (2001), a cultural geographer, warns in his article summarizing landscape studies, "No longer is localism, no matter how contextualized, sufficient" (p. 270). The limitations he perceives in a narrow study of the local have often been avoided in my classroom, in large part because of the creativity and enthusiasm the students have shown once they become real research writers of the communities in their region.

I now ask my students repeatedly, throughout the semester, Putnam's (2000) question about how a person can participate effectively in the public life of a community. When students understand that "history has a fundamental relevance to contemporary public policy" (Jackson, 1985, p. 4) and that "the history of urban [or local, regional, or global] cultural landscapes offer citizens and public officials some basis for making political and spatial choices about the future" (Hayden, 1999, p. 43), then they are empowered through this understanding and enact it through writing. As students examine the spaces around them, they find the histories of many forces layered in their landscape. Their local examination provides a much-needed bridge to global awareness as they recognize more fully the interconnected nature of our world. Students as composers of many communities within and beyond our classroom realize that our work doesn't stop at the doorway at the end of the semester, as it once did. With that in mind, Josie, in an online posting, advised her classmates to find something or someplace they cared about and make themselves known. And they have done just that.

REFERENCES

Anderson, B. (1991). *Imagined communities: Reflections on the origin and spread of nationalism* (Rev. ed.). New York: Verso Books.

Austin, M. (1987). The basket maker. In Melody Graulich (Ed.), *Western trails: A collection of short stories* (pp. 31–35). Reno: University of Nevada Press.

Ballenger, B. (2001). *The curious researcher* (3rd ed.). Boston: Allyn & Bacon.

Bishop, W., & Zemliansky, P. (2001). *The subject is research: Processes and practices*. Portsmouth, NH: Boynton-Cook.

Chiseri-Strater, E., & Sunstein, B. (1997). Researching place: The spatial gaze. In *FieldWorking: Reading and writing research*. Upper Saddle River, NJ: Prentice Hall.

Garreau, J. (1992). *Edge city: Life on the new frontier*. New York: Anchor.

Hart, E. L. (1996). Literacy and the lesbian/gay learner. In S. Garnes et al. (Eds.), *Writing lives: Exploring literacy and community* (pp. 121–132). New York: St. Martin's Press.

Hayden, D. (1999). *The power of place: Urban landscapes as public history*. Cambridge, MA: MIT Press.

Jackson, K. T. (1985). *Crabgrass frontier: The suburbanization of the United States*. New York: Oxford University Press.

Johnson, J. (1992). *The Bedford guide to the research process* (2nd ed.). Boston: Bedford Books/St. Martin's Press.

Lippard, L. (1997) *The lure of the local: Senses of place in a multicentered society*. New York: New Press.

Marshall, I., & Ryden, W. (2000). Interrogating the monologue: Making Whiteness visible. *CCC: College composition and communication, 52*, 240–259.

Mitchell, D. (2001). The lure of the local: Landscape studies at the end of a troubled century. *Progress in human geography, 25*(2), 270. Retrieved January 27, 2003, from http://galileo.usg.edu

Putnam, R. (2000). *Bowling alone: The collapse and revival of American community.* New York: Simon & Schuster.

Rand, L. A. (2001) Enacting faith: Evangelical discourse and the discipline of composition studies. *CCC: College Composition and Communication, 52,* 349–367.

Rhoades, G., & Sanders, L. M. (2001). Creating knowledge through primary research. In Bishop, W., & Zemliansky, P. (Eds.), *The subject is research: Processes and practices* (pp. 69–81). Portsmouth, NH: Heinemann.

Zagarell, S. (1988). Narrative of community: The identification of a genre. *Signs, 13,* 498.

PART II

Public Literacy Projects and Civic Culture

As illustrated in Part I, bringing "community" into the classroom changes that social space. However, another significant dimension of "community studies" emerges when students and teachers extend their cultural work beyond typical classroom boundaries, by purposefully disseminating their learning to public audiences and actively participating in civic life.

Recurring themes in this section point to the impact that students' collaborative literacy practices can have on the larger culture. At the same time, these essays emphasize benefits that students and teachers themselves can gain from engaging with public issues, initiating extra projects, and sharing their learning with diverse audiences. Thus, you will see students, teachers, and stakeholders from the larger community collaborating in civic action to build new knowledge and address authentic social issues. You will also find powerful examples of classroom research and writing being cast into "public genres" (such as live performances and Web site writing) strategically selected to address community-related questions. Along the way, as the walls that usually separate classroom life from community culture dissolve, students become "rhetors" in the classical sense— using language to seek and enable social change.

We realize that ambitious agendas for civic engagement may, at first, appear as daunting as they are inspiring. So while this section's authors all celebrate major projects involving multiple stakeholders, the writers also work to show you some of the early classroom-based experiments they tried and the gradual steps they took with students before attempting their larger endeavors. In whatever way you begin this work, we believe, the benefits to all are significant, since public literacy projects promote civic culture, preparing students for active citizenship and lifelong learning.

CHAPTER 8

Learning to Write as a Community: Embracing Collaborative Process and Product

Traci Blanchard

Writing is integral to both keeping and creating our communities. This guiding principle has been demonstrated repeatedly throughout the work of the Keeping and Creating American Communities (KCAC) project, and nowhere has its power been felt more profoundly than in the execution of our project's Web site. When the project began in the summer of 2000, I accepted the charge of leading our efforts to encapsulate KCAC's story on the Web. I had previously designed Web sites for a variety of academic purposes, with my projects including an informational site for my high school's language arts department and an online literary magazine. However, I could never have anticipated that the work I would do on the KCAC Web site would so enrich my own classroom community and the writing my students produced. The lessons the KCAC Web team learned about collaborative writing, ownership, and the distinction between product and process have extended far beyond the space of the World Wide Web, enlightening our teaching and writing in ways we had not dreamed of. My work with KCAC, as well as in my own classroom, has convinced me of the need for collaboration in keeping and creating our communities and of the power a meaningful research process creates.

BUILDING THE KCAC WEBSITE

From the beginning, the design of the Web site was a collaborative effort. Planning included the project directors, Mimi Dyer and Sarah Robbins, and focused initially on the ways in which the Web could best serve our needs. We saw the Web as a relatively inexpensive, extraordinarily accessible tool for dissemination. We wanted to make our research and methodology available to a wide audience of educators and students, to provide access to hard-to-find information, and to open the way to a process of research and recovery so that others might be inspired to attempt similar work for themselves, in their own communities.

Once the KCAC project was under way, the entire group of teacher participants and team leaders became involved in the Web site's design and content. With such a complex site, so many components, and the lack of a clear model to guide us, collaboration was key to accomplishing an effective design. Every aspect of the site was reviewed, critiqued, and refined so that the final product represented not only KCAC research, but also, as nearly as possible, the KCAC experience itself. Minute details, such as the selection of pictures for the splash image and the choice of fonts, were discussed and debated until we achieved a form that the entire KCAC team could be excited about.

The final Web site (see Figure 8.1) is organized into a few distinct sections: Curricular Program, Thematic Content, Classroom Resources, and Community Projects. These sections reflect the multifaceted nature of the project as a whole and provide a framework for the incredible projects that teacher participants and their students generated using KCAC strategies and principles.

The Curricular Program section details the educational basis of the KCAC model and describes professional development opportunities for other teachers. Thematic Content offers academic resource material derived from our teacher participants' KCAC research experiences. Classroom Resources provides an extensive collection of lesson plans that were generated through teachers' KCAC participation. Community Projects showcases those aspects of KCAC that moved beyond classroom boundaries and brought together students, teachers, and community members in their efforts to recover, celebrate, and preserve American communities.

The collaborative principles of KCAC are mirrored in the final Web site. My role in its creation was multifaceted. On the one hand, I was a learner actively engaged in discovering how to compress the entire project into a Web resource. On the other, I was a teacher, instructing fellow teacher participants in how to create Web-friendly text, how to use a variety of software and technology, and how to determine what exactly was possible to portray through the Web medium. Finally, I was an audience, eager to see what these teachers and their students would create when allowed to let the research itself define the form their final products would take. By guiding this team in the collaborative creation of the Web site, I

Keeping and Creating
American Communities

a project funded in part by the National Endowment for the Humanities

Curricular
Program

Thematic
Content

Classroom
Resources

Community
Projects

Who
We Are

Welcome!

KCAC invites educators from all subject areas, grade levels, and school environments to study and to shape American communities.

This website introduces educators and community members to a model for interdisciplinary learning developed in a <u>multi-year project</u> funded by the <u>National Endowment for the Humanities</u> (NEH). Over several years, <u>teachers</u> affiliated with the <u>National Writing Project</u> created this <u>curricular program</u> for teaching collaboratively about American communities.

The program promotes student research and writing to explore community life. Through <u>community projects</u> and collaborative research, **KCAC** supports students' and teachers' interactions with community members. These collaborations expand the study of local cultures to reflect the increasing diversity evident in American life.

Figure 8.1. Excerpt from home page for the KCAC Web site.

unknowingly started on a new path that would result in dramatic changes in my own secondary classroom.

THE VIRTUAL WORLD: EXPLORATION

Being open to multiple, varied products is often difficult—for both the teacher and the student. As students, we like to know what's expected of us—we want a blueprint, a color-by-numbers assignment that we can simply plug our data into and be rewarded with the big A. As teachers, we know that we are much more likely to get what we want if we present several examples—the more explicit our instructions and detailed our illustrations, the more likely we'll receive products that meet our expectations. So what happens when we let go, when we open ourselves to the possibilities of multiple, varied products?

From KCAC's inception, I began scheming and planning, attempting to take in all the many varied elements of this multilayered research and writing initiative, and blend them into a cohesive whole that would provide much-needed resource material for educators. And from the beginning, the teacher participants asked me, "What *exactly* do you want for the Web site?" It was a difficult, indeed impossible, question to answer. The content of community studies, in and of itself, is always changing, always unpredictable. I had no way of knowing what the teachers' research would uncover, so how could I possibly know what form their final products should take? Part of the excitement of authentic research is this very uncertainty. What the other teacher participants and I learned through our work was to be patient, to live with the uncertainty, and to let the content dictate the form of the final products. I believe that our lack of prescriptive models made what we eventually received from our teachers much richer than anything we might have anticipated. Additionally, the collaborative basis of the project was integral to the creation of the rich, varied products now showcased on the Web. The combination of collaboration and ownership allowed these teacher researchers and their students a freedom seldom afforded by academic endeavors.

One example of how content dictated form and how collaboration creates power is visible in Bonnie Webb's virtual tour of the Martin Luther King, Jr., Center and historic site in Atlanta, Georgia (Webb, 2002). This project married many elements of what makes technology and the Web effective teaching tools: deceptively simple activities that generate productive results. Bonnie's students analyzed museum exhibits and then responded to writing prompts that encouraged them to analyze what they had seen. Now, on the Web site, striking images combine with student writing in a PowerPoint presentation that is its own teaching tool now accessible to any teacher with Web access. Also powerful is how the project demonstrates the possibilities for student-teacher collaboration, as teacher design and student writing combine with powerful resonance. Had we initially provided Bonnie with a prescriptive form, it seems unlikely she and her students would have responded in this innovative way. And yet her virtual tour features community research through student writing, cutting right to the heart of KCAC's guiding principles in a way that may inspire other, similar projects across the country.

Another unique product that emerged from the KCAC research was Linda Stewart's examination of planned suburban communities in her essay "The Town Square Redux?" (Stewart, 2002). While this essay is ascribed to a single author, the research was definitely a collaborative effort. Charged with the study of suburbia, the Shifting Landscapes, Converging Peoples group of teacher participants visited a number of communities *as a team*. Throughout their field research, the members of the team refined and developed the questions that drove Linda's inquiry, making this article the product of collaboration as well as individual authorship. In her article, Linda critically examines the idea of a planned community designed to re-create the nostalgia of a small town. The revelation that the apartment community had created its own *fictional* history illustrates our need for a sense of belonging. As Linda so eloquently observes, "The production and design of Post Riverside is a reproduction of the past in bricks and ink. It's not real, but it does reveal. By examining planned communities across America, we can better understand the nature of Americans, their neighborhoods, their dreams, and their communities" (Stewart, 2002).

The Educating for Citizenship thematic section provides yet another example of collaborative research. Allowing team members to focus on their individual areas of expertise led to the creation of diverse and complementary final products. The topic centered on the cross-racial partnerships that helped establish Spelman College in Atlanta and the important civic work of its early graduates. Researchers were fortunate to find a rich resource in the college's archives. Perhaps more than for any other team, the research for this strand demanded digging through archives, a time-consuming but ultimately rewarding task. As team member Ed Hullender (2000–2001) observed, "Good historical teaching is about connecting with the past. Using historical documents affords all of us the opportunity to delve into the past in a meaningful and positive way." However, other components of this section of the Web site use oral histories and photography to contribute to KCAC's compelling glimpse into this time period. Supporting the team's writing, Kennesaw State University interns were integral to the process of editing Web content, transcribing and scanning various documents loaned by Spelman's archivist, and designing the eventual Web pages that demonstrate the power of teamwork—in both the Spelman and KCAC communities.

THE REAL WORLD: MY CLASSROOM

My experiences with teamwork in building the KCAC Web site showed me time and again the value of collaboration in keeping and creating community, as well as the energy that meaningful research generates. I wanted to share these experiences with my own students. Therefore, with these ideals in mind, I revamped my senior project, changing it into one that required my students to participate in collaborative, community-based research. Having witnessed my colleagues' excitement as they delved into primary sources in a variety of forms, I wanted to offer my students the same opportunities for authentic research. Additionally, I saw this project as an invitation to my students to become active participants, involved citizens, in their local community.

For many years I have taught honors seniors at Lassiter High School, a large, primarily White, affluent community located in a suburb of Atlanta. Almost all my students go on to college, many to prestigious universities across the nation. These students grow up to become doctors, lawyers, educators—many become leaders in their respective fields. As high school seniors, however, most feel that their connection to and impact on their local community is minimal at best. With this project, I wanted these high achievers to understand early on that their voices were already important, that they could make a difference.

My idealism, however, is grounded in practicality: Our county curriculum requires that senior students complete a formal research paper. With increasingly easy access to the Internet, plagiarism and sheer academic laziness seemed to have reduced the research process for my seniors into an exercise in cutting and pasting. I became more and more concerned with having my students conduct relevant research that forced them to move beyond their computer screens and library shelves and into the communities they can help shape even now.

The students chose three- or four-person research teams, not far different from the teacher teams we used in KCAC. When KCAC began, teacher participants identified themes they were most interested in researching, and team leaders used these preferences to determine team assignments. Similarly, my students and I spent a few days discussing local issues, my hope being that students would form their groups based on common interest in a given topic.

Each team was charged with researching an issue that was having an impact on our local community, but their process could not stop there. Additionally, an outcome of their research had to be a proposal for a possible solution to the problem or legitimate public response to the issue. Students had to become personally, actively involved. Consistent with the KCAC model, these teams were educating themselves for citizenship in their local communities. Finally, each research team was required to produce two research products incorporating both graphics and text. As for KCAC teachers' writing for our Web site, the concept of the product was open, though each student had to fully illustrate the research and demonstrate mastery of Modern Language Association documentation. None of the products could be in the form of a traditional research paper.

Critical to my students' selection of the forms of their final products was a consideration of audience. Unlike the traditional high school research paper with its audience of one—the teacher—these products had to be targeted to a broader, specific audience, forcing students to consider from the beginning who would benefit from their research. If my students thought their writing might find a real-world audience, I believed they would be more committed to the research process and imbued with a sense of purpose often missing from writing directed only to the teacher.

Giving students the opportunity to decide on the best format for their research was a little scary, and it created its own advantages and disadvantages. On the plus side, students felt ownership from the beginning because of the high level of choice. Students chose their own teams, their own issues to be researched, and their own product formats. As a result, the research process itself was exciting for both my students and me. Most groups selected issues in which they had a personal interest, such as cuts in the local school budget, the proposed sale and demolition of a local climbing area to a high-dollar developer, pollution in the Chattahoochee River (the major water source for metro Atlanta), and the economic impact of 9/11 on the city.

This type of research demanded personal interviews, as well as on-site visits, so my students quickly began to feel vested in the importance of their research. Instead of merely reading other writers' opinions and conclusions about their topics, my students were doing firsthand research that forced them to generate their own opinions, to draw their own conclusions. As the research progressed, I monitored their progress in a variety of ways. I circulated during group discussions in class, offering suggestions and gaining valuable insight into the progress each team was making. I conducted individual research checks to ensure that each student was carrying his or her weight in contributing to the body of the group's resources. I also required each student to complete a separate report of either a personal interview or an on-site visit. These checkpoints allowed me to see for myself that my students were engaged and enthusiastic about this new approach to an age-old curricular requirement.

I left the depth of collaboration and the form of the final research products up to the students. Having taught honors courses for many years, I predicted that a few students would resist collaborating on the final product, being unwilling to risk their GPAs, so I had allowed the option of individual work. To my surprise, all my students chose to collaborate with at least one other team member.

Several of the products were outstanding. Letters to congresspeople and school board members, Web pages, PowerPoint presentations, and video documentaries were just a few of the creative outcomes. Their research on pollution in the Chattahoochee River led the members of one group to develop an extraordinary Web site that not only detailed the problem, but also presented commonsense steps that each of us could take to improve the quality of this essential natural resource. Letters to local lawmakers presented well-reasoned, well-researched, eloquent appeals for help on a variety of issues, including stricter enforcement of laws banning cigarette sales to minors and continued funding of music education programs. PowerPoint presentations detailed the local economic impact of 9/11 and the reasons behind recent school budget cuts.

Perhaps the most impressive result came from the topic that initially I had had the least faith in, primarily because of the lack of published information via the Internet or print materials. One of my students, Dwayne, was an avid climber passionately interested in the controversy surrounding a bouldering area just outside of Atlanta. The property, known as Boat Rock, had been basically abandoned, and for years it had provided a climbing haven for die-hard boulderers. However, a big-name builder with deep pockets had targeted the area for a new subdivision. In fact, one area of the million-year-old boulders had already been destroyed to make way for new half-million-dollar homes. A local climbing association had taken up the charge and was campaigning vigorously to purchase the land, holding fund-raisers and rallies, trying desperately to increase public awareness of the natural resource that was about to be destroyed in the name of progress. Dwayne convinced his team members that this issue could be the focus of their research. His two teammates knew nothing about climbing, so first he became their teacher, helping them to understand the basics and the lingo before they could begin the true research.

What followed was a shining example of authentic research. These students were unable to rely on print sources for their information, particularly since things were happening so fast that print sources were often inaccurate. Instead, the group conducted interview after interview, attended rallies and fund-raising events, and created a video documentary that is amazing not only for its technical skill, but also for its chronicle of this rapidly changing chapter of local history. These students became so invested that they spent the afternoon before their senior prom capturing just a bit more of the area on video—they wanted their final product to be as complete and up-to-date as it could possibly be. In the end, the climbers' association won. Their bid for the property was accepted, and they continue to raise money to pay for the mortgage on Boat Rock. My students' excitement at being a part of a successful grassroots effort was just as important as the documentary that I will share with future classes for years to come.

All these students' research products included the necessary "call to action": They reached outside their research groups to other students, to their community, and to public-policy makers to request change, often providing well-thought-out options for that change. Giving students the opportunity to connect in a meaningful way with their community, as well as showing them that their voices are important and that there are audiences eager to hear those voices, empowers our young people and prepares them for active citizenship, an educational outcome far beyond mastery of research skills.

ANALYSIS AND IMPLICATIONS

I do have to be honest: Some of the final products did not adequately illustrate the incredible research process I had witnessed throughout the project. While some groups produced impressively polished final products, some did not. Initially, I was a bit disappointed. How could the same project, the same level of instruction, yield such vastly different results?

Gradually, I realized that because my students had so much choice, because there were no templates or models on which to base their final products, the overall quality of their research products was bound to be uneven. Unlike my KCAC colleagues, these students did not have advanced degrees or years of professional experience. They were not published authors or award-winning educators. Instead, they were simply teenagers embracing the research process and learning about collaboration and research strategies along the way.

After reviewing the students' research process and the products as a whole, I realized that the success of the project was based more on the foundation of collaboration than on the final products. While I feel that all my students gained from the research process, those who embraced its collaborative nature and opportunities were ultimately happier with their research experience and produced more successful final products. In my concern for accountability, both mine and my students', I myself lost sight of the crucial element that had led me to this project in the first place: the value of collaborative community research.

Throughout our work in KCAC, we have seen again and again how collaboration enriches our lives, our research, and our writing. With KCAC, we were educated professionals who had 2½ years to develop and refine this process of collaboration into finished products. My poor students were allotted a mere 10 weeks. In spite of this limitation and my own lack of specific instruction in how to accomplish collaborative research and writing, many of my students excelled. Those students were eager for the opportunity to share the work, not because it was easier, but because it was more: more exciting, more in-depth, and more satisfying. In their assessments of the project as a whole, most were overwhelmingly positive about the fact that their research seemed meaningful and relevant; that they enjoyed working within a team toward a common end; and that they felt the group-defined products were superior, though ultimately more time-consuming, to the typical paper as a measure of their research.

Some of the groups who struggled with the collaborative model commented that they wished their group had shared components of its research more fully along the way. Naively, I had assumed that they would do so without my prompting. The next time I embark on this project with my own students, I will guide them more explicitly by leading them through a loose model of the process while still allowing them to define and create their own products.

Regardless of the variations in their final products, almost all my students were actively and enthusiastically engaged in community research. High school seniors in their final semester developed social consciousness as they became involved in learning more about the community in which they live and the issues that affect it. Many of my students discovered passions for causes that before had seemed remote or unimportant. The group who researched pollution in the Chattahoochee River became impassioned protectors of this natural resource, as evidenced in their earnest appeals to classmates to conserve water and use common sense to prevent further pollution. One young woman, whose group had researched school budget cuts, was so incensed by her findings that she felt empowered to directly question our state's governor at a function just a few weeks following the project's completion. Her passion could only have been born out of her immersion in her research.

Of the team that studied the potential destruction of Boat Rock, only one was a climber at the outset. By the end, all the team members had become avid, energetic advocates and had begun developing a passion for the sport of climbing. Perhaps more remarkable, the group's astonishing video was completed *after* the product's due date. These students became so committed to creating a quality documentary that they chose to substitute another, less ambitious product for grading so that they could take the extra time necessary to bring to fruition the vision they had for their video.

Outcomes such as these become possible when students feel ownership of the process *and* the product, when they are given the opportunity to engage in research that is meaningful and relevant to their lives and the community in which they live. When schoolwork becomes life work, remarkable learning results.

In the end, my role as Webmaster and my role as teacher were not so very different. My work with KCAC and my students has taught me to embrace the research process as well as the product. The community connection and authentic inquiry that the KCAC teachers and my students embraced were invaluable—worthwhile beyond the immediate dissemination of their research. Had we provided prescriptive models to these teachers and students, the end results would no doubt have been more consistent with our initial standards and expectations. And yet what would we have lost? The creativity and originality exhibited by both my students and my KCAC colleagues is only possible in an environment that invites ownership and experimentation, that is, in a classroom or Web community that celebrates those who dare to take risks.

REFERENCES

Hullender, E. (2000–2001). Doing archival research. In *Keeping and creating American communities*. Retrieved March 2, 2004, from http://kcac.kennesaw.edu/thematic_content/educating_for_citizenship/archival.html

Stewart, L. (2002). The town square redux? In *Keeping and creating American communities*. Retrieved March 2, 2004, from http://kcac.kennesaw.edu/thematic_content/shifting_landscapes_converging_peoples/redux.html

Webb, B. (2002). MLK, Jr., Center: A virtual tour. In *Keeping and Creating American communities*. Retrieved March 2, 2004, from http://kcac.kennesaw.edu/thematic_content/building_cities/buihome.html

CHAPTER 9

Writing a Museum

Bonnie Webb

Keeping and Creating American Communities (KCAC) teachers believe that what a community elects to keep, or in some cases destroy, provides valuable insight into local culture. We also believe that our students often do not have the same sense of community as other generations, and that it's not their fault. Students didn't decide where their families lived. They didn't decide to tear down century-old buildings in order to build condos. They didn't decide to destroy a neighborhood to build a baseball stadium. Others did such things, and our students were the innocent witnesses to the destruction. KCAC participants share the idea that we, as educators, need to help our students learn the meaning of community—both past and present.

In the first year of the KCAC program, the two dozen teacher participants divided into smaller research teams organized around the KCAC themes. When our group first met, we selected the national "Building Cities" theme that focuses on how American cities can be considered artifacts of their community's culture. The local application of "Re-imagining Atlanta as a Cultural, Corporate Center," with emphasis on how Atlanta was consciously transformed from a regional to a national center in the 1970s and 1980s, helped guide us through the first year.

Our task was to research these themes and to share what we learned with other teachers and students. When one group member lobbied to research Atlanta's High Museum of Art, we started to focus on city museums and monuments. Our group began visiting the sites that our area had to offer. We also "visited" online museums located in other cities and agreed that each of us would research particular museums in Atlanta with our students during the school year.

Writing America: Classroom Literacy and Public Engagement. Copyright © 2005 by Teachers College, Columbia University. All rights reserved. ISBN 0-8077-4527-8 (pbk). Prior to photocopying items for classroom use, please contact the Copyright Clearance Center, Customer Service, 222 Rosewood Dr., Danvers, MA 01923, USA, tel. (508) 750-8400.

Selecting a research topic was not an easy choice for me. Atlanta offers a myriad of sites that define the culture of our city. When most people think of Atlanta, the Civil War and *Gone with the Wind* come to mind; however, these are only a part of our city's rich heritage. Several of our KCAC research experiences demonstrated that Atlanta is a city of very diverse cultures that blend the old and the new. A KCAC walking tour of Atlanta led by a professor of urban studies and American Studies featured both historic and contemporary Atlanta—the old architecture of Atlanta is often dwarfed by the new, but some history remains. Also, our visit to the William Breman Jewish Heritage Museum helped dispel the common notion that Atlanta is an "all-Baptist" culture. Team member Dave Winter (2000–2001) and his high school students investigated the Atlanta Zoo and the CNN Center, both dynamic landmarks that have seen decades of change.

My students who were involved in this project were advanced-content language arts and social studies eighth graders in a suburban middle school outside Atlanta. The population is diverse, with 40% White, 40% African American, 10% Hispanic, and 10% other. This diversity did not, however, influence how I chose the site for our inquiry. Rather, I looked for a site that would be interesting, extend the required curriculum, fit county guidelines for travel, and provide enough information for good writing prompts for advanced students. I realized that I would need to do some museum studies of my own before involving my students. I needed to choose an appropriate site, research its history, and prepare appropriate instructional materials to support student writings and reflections.

I selected the Martin Luther King, Jr., Center for Non-violent Social Change because it provided a wide-angle view of both the work of Dr. King and the civil rights movement. Also, our eighth-grade Georgia studies curriculum includes objectives in this area. My own research confirmed that the King Center would be a great opportunity for my students to learn about values important to our community and the nation.

Mrs. Coretta Scott King created the original King Center for Non-Violent Social Change in 1968 to be both an official and living memorial to the work of Dr. King. More than 650,000 visitors from around the world visit the center each year. The center houses the final resting place of Dr. King and archives from the movement and illustrates his life and teachings.

The site was named a historic district in May 1974, and gained national park status on October 10, 1980. Auburn Avenue, home to both the King Center and the Birthplace, was a thriving center of African American culture and business during the 1930s and 1940s. Early civil rights advocate John Wesley Dobbs dubbed the street "Sweet Auburn" because it offered Blacks opportunities not afforded them in most areas of the South.

The "sweet" represented the money generated on the street. It remains home to several African American institutions, such as the first Black-owned daily newspaper, the *Atlanta Daily World*, founded by W. A. Scott in 1928, and the Ebenezer Baptist Church, founded by Reverend John Parker in 1886.

In *Atlanta Rising*, Frederick Allen (1996) describes the Black businesses on the street, which included restaurants, stores, theaters, and a bank. Here former slave Alonzo Herndon turned his Peachtree Street barbershop profits into Atlanta Life, an insurance company exclusively for Blacks. By the 1940s the company was worth more than 12 million dollars in assets and had branches in nine states (p. 36).

During the 1960s and early 1970s the Auburn area businesses closed and residents began to move away. In *Where Peachtree Meets Sweet Auburn*, Gary Pomerantz (1996) describes Auburn Avenue as a "decaying memorial to a bygone era" (p. 485). Maynard Jackson, the first Black mayor elected in a major southern city and grandson of John Wesley Dobbs, devised a revitalization plan that originally did not have positive results. But the designation of Auburn Avenue as an official historic district in December of 1976 gave hope that the area would rise again. Today, a diverse crowd can be found on the street, illustrating former mayor Jackson's observation that "Auburn Avenue was a living lab for King's dreams" (CNN Interactive–U.S. News, 1998).

I visited the King Center twice before bringing my students there, to familiarize myself with the center and to gather writing prompts. I also collected images to create a virtual field trip in case my students were unable to go in person. Each visit presented a different crowd, creating a different atmosphere each time.

My first trip to the King Center was early on a Sunday morning. I was surprised at the crowd. On Sundays Atlanta is a "church town" that doesn't see crowds until after morning services. On this visit, the audience was predominately senior African Americans on charter tours from all over the country. This was generally a quiet, almost somber group that took the time to read everything. Several had tears in their eyes at Dr. King's gravesite. When they posed for pictures in front of the gravesite and the different displays, they assumed a serious stance and expression. They remembered Dr. King and, because of their age, I presume, had experienced firsthand the struggles of the civil rights movement.

The crowd on my second visit was more racially diverse and a lot younger. They skimmed through the exhibits, mainly looking at the photographs. They were a respectful but more lighthearted group that smiled for their photos in front of the gravesite. They hadn't lived through the times experienced by the senior group. Now I wish that I had taken the time to talk with the visitors at the center during these visits. I'm sure that they all had stories to tell. Watching the behaviors of these two different groups of visitors helped me better prepare my students for their trip, because I was able to explain that we were going to visit a place of both celebration and sorrow and that their behavior should take both into consideration.

STUDENT WRITING AT SCHOOL AND AT THE CENTER

From the beginning of this project, the Building Cities group decided to fully include our students. Students, told that they were part of KCAC, were given a brief synopsis of what happened at meetings, read e-mails that shared information, and visited the KCAC Web site. These KCAC students (for that is how they viewed themselves) and my team teacher, Sandra Grant, deserve a lot of credit for the wonderful writing.

The King Center for Non-violent Social Change houses the files, offices, and personal memorabilia of the King family and Mahatma Gandhi. Our spring 2001 writing excursion took place mainly in the visitor's center. I selected this part of the site because of its interactive displays, videos, statues, news stories, photographs of the movement, and two videos that best told the story.

The visitor's center is designed to be an interactive experience for the guests. On entering, you see center displays that explain topics such as segregation and the Freedom Fighters and features of other movements. "Discovery Drawers" explain the culture of the 1960s. Visitors young and old enjoy opening the doors and drawers to read the information and view the images. My students were amused at the fashions, hairstyles, and 45-rpm records in the Discovery Drawers. For me it was a glimpse into my past.

The civil rights story is explained in sections located around a center walk with statues of human figures marching toward a large window that overlooks the gardens. The figures on the walk reflect the diversity of the people in the movement. While on the walkway, students looked down to read the list of prominent civil rights organizations and events.

Clustered around the walkway are six areas that explain the civil rights movement of the 1960s. All six areas contain images, information, artifacts, and closed-caption videos under the topics "Segregation," "The King Family," "Call to Lead," "Visiting the Mountain," "Expanding the Dream," and "Overcoming Loss." Most of the images are in black and white, a color scheme that is often not appreciated by the age group that I took to the site. This was not the case at the center. Students such as Emily even commented in their evaluations that viewing the story only in black and white added to the images' powerful impact:

> The Martin Luther King Jr. Museum is a very strong and powerful place. Right when you walk in you can see all of the information. It isn't just a place where you simply read the information; rather, it is a place that you can really interact and understand what black people went through. When you see the pictures on the walls, you wonder how some people can be so cruel and uncaring. Understanding and actually seeing what people had to face back then really makes you think about how you too can make a difference. (Emily)

The writing prompts for the student packet were designed to accommodate good to excellent eighth-grade writers. We reviewed the student packet twice before our visit, and the packets were distributed to the students as they boarded the bus to the center. They included images from the center, a brief guide to the site, and a list of varied writing prompts designed to make the students think about what they were seeing. Two notes to the students, highlighted and discussed several times, encouraged them to use different genres of writing and to include personal opinions. I wanted them to have some control over their writing, yet I needed to provide some guidance to keep them thinking. The students did indeed write in varied genres, including poetry, diary entries, historical fiction, narrative, and a newspaper article. They indicated later that having the freedom of choice made them believe that they were part of the process, not just the product. They felt that they were actually helping to write lesson plans for future classes.

The greatest volume of student writing came from the civil rights photo gallery. A series of black-and-white pictures lines the back wall of the center, depicting significant moments from the movement. Encompassing works from photographers such as Charles Moore and Charmaine Chaplan Reading, the images display the wide range of emotions, challenges, violence, and success stories from the civil rights movement of the 1960s. For this section of the packet, I supplied questions to help guide, but not dictate, student writing. Some of the questions included, What is the focal point? Why did the photographer select that point? What events preceded this photograph? What happened after the image was captured? What story does the image tell? My students wrote some excellent reflective pieces that expressed their shock and dismay that these incidents took place in their country and almost in their own backyards.

Ashley selected a titled photograph of two Black people being taunted and physically threatened by an angry group of Whites. She stated in her reflection that she felt the reason the photograph was not centered was that the angry crowd jostled the photographer.

Feeling the Hate

Feeling yourself being shoved out of the doors of a "whites only" restaurant
Looking around to see crowds of angry people glaring at you with degrading eyes
Hearing cruel words coming from those who despise you
Sensing the hate, the hate that seems to be everywhere swallowing you up
Running from the men that are beating you with immense force
Protecting yourself from the bats and sticks being swung at you
Praying for the strength, the strength to keep going
Fearing what is happening, and what is yet to come
Crying tears, tears full of sorrow and pain

Hoping it will end and that no one else will have to endure the same

There was no assignment that all students had to do. Choices were available in all areas of the packet. For example, students were asked to select and describe an image from the gallery, but they had many images to choose from, because the King Center divides its story into six display areas. Sample writing prompts from the packet included the following:

- The Freedom Riders: Who were they? What was their mission? Were they successful?
- Describe the role of the media in the civil rights movement. How did they help? How did they hurt?
- Compare and contrast the views of Dr. King with those of another civil rights leader.
- After viewing the gravesite area, write your reaction(s) to the site.

After lunch at the Varsity, an Atlanta landmark restaurant, students returned to school for their extended writing time. I had arranged for students to use the school computer lab for the 1½ hours left in the school day. Each student discussed and wrote for all but the last 15 minutes, which were reserved for voluntary sharing. Students handed me their saved work on a disk before leaving. Although I also planned a revision session for the following day, I knew that it was important for students to write while the experience was still fresh.

STUDENTS BECOMING MUSEUM GUIDES

Early in the project I had begun to collect images in case we could not make the trip in person. My initial goal was to create a virtual tour of the site. On my introductory visits I began taking digital photographs from the time I stepped on the grounds. The collection of images was greatly enhanced by a student photographer who was selected to make the trip with us. I showed my class the images during their revision time the day after our visit. They thought that it was a good idea to complete the virtual tour anyway, so that students from other parts of the country could visit the center online. Field trips are increasingly hard to arrange, so virtual tours are becoming the way to go. Visit our virtual tour at http://kcac.kennesaw.edu/thematic_content/powerpoints/mlk.ppt

The King Center virtual tour was the first one I constructed with students as co-authors. My experience with KCAC showed me that the students are of valuable help in creating tours relevant to their age group. I plan to include them more often and encourage them to create virtual PowerPoint tours after visiting historic or other interesting places.

One possible obstacle to creating virtual tours is that taking photographs is prohibited at some sites. At the King Center, flash photography was allowed everywhere except at the King birth home. Art museums are particularly averse to flash photography, as are many historic homes, such as Monticello and Montpelier. Copyright violations and eventual damage from the flash are the major reasons for banning flash photography in some places.

After most of the images were selected, the students made suggestions for appropriate captions; we then combined the images and captions into a PowerPoint presentation. Once again I was faced with the decision of how much information we should include. Would this tour be designed for those who could not make it to the site in person? Or should it be designed as an introduction for those who may visit the site? My students decided that it should be a combination of both. After three small-group editing sessions, we felt that the end product could be used as a general introduction and supply enough information for those who would not be able to visit in person.

The experience at the King Center was a success. Students and parents sent e-mails and stopped by the classroom to give compliments. Even more important, the students produced high-quality work because they had some control. Since I was not following any canned or commercial lesson plans, we were literally "writing the book" on this activity. The students were eager to suggest changes, corrections, and enhancements, which were often incorporated into both the project and the end products. For instance, they suggested cutting back on the captions and letting the images tell more of the story. They also thought they needed more time to visit the center, so perhaps next time we will view the documentary of the civil rights movement prior to the visit, instead of taking the time to view it at the site.

ANALYSIS AND IMPLICATIONS

I learned from this experience that a teacher must decide how much prior knowledge is necessary for effective student writing without spoiling the experience. I did not provide the students with much information on the civil rights movement or the Jim Crow laws prior to our visit to the center. While compiling the student packet, I wondered if this would be a mistake, but it proved to be a good strategy. The students were shocked at the displays showing separate schools, restaurants, and restrooms. I feel that since they were not overprepared for this part of the visit, they paid closer attention to the displays and generated exceptional writing because of this "new" experience. One young man in our group was shocked at the scene of Dr. King in a jail cell. He could not believe that a man like King would have been jailed for trying to free people from segregation. He spent a good portion of his visit at this display explaining the story to the other students, and this one image became the focal point of his writing.

The student packet seemed to provide a good guide for the students. The prompts suggested opportunities that resulted in a diverse collection of writings. Future packets will include a timeline for the day, more information on the Auburn Historic District, and a little more information on how to navigate the museum. For my weaker writers I included an option of creating a timeline on the life of Dr. King or the civil rights movement. I would not include such options in the future, because several of my better writers elected to do this rather than the higher-level writing prompts, so I plan to "raise the bar" on future trips by eliminating this type of writing prompt.

Adapting "Writing a Museum" to other sites in other cities would easily fit the plan used at the King Center. Recently, in New Orleans, I visited the D-Day Museum, an excellent candidate for a virtual field trip. Most of the displays were created with personal artifacts donated by both

American and German participants. Personal histories from members of the military and civilians from both sides tell the story of this part of history. A collection of images can be used to create online virtual tours and technology presentations for other classes or to enhance student writing. Preliminary teacher visitation is essential in order to create a series of writing prompts, to establish a guide or plan, and to determine how much prior knowledge of the site is needed for a successful visit.

When students are invited to examine a site by thinking, evaluating, reflecting, and then responding to what they see, they are able to better understand why that particular site is important to local culture. When students visit a site that their community has chosen to preserve, they view the information and the manner in which the space is presented, thus enabling them to identify with the values behind the drive to protect a particular slice of local culture. When students are invited to go beyond "visiting," they begin to move from observation to genuine social consciousness. Then students can move to becoming future curators of their culture.

Because of the nature of this research, reflection, and writing activity, it should not matter if students have already seen the landmark before. "Writing a Museum" will make them see it in a different light and help them move from the role of passive observers to that of active participants in the preservation of their community.

REFERENCES

Allen, F. (1996). *Atlanta rising*. Marietta, GA: Longstreet Press.

CNN Interactive-U.S. News. (1998). Atlanta's King's Sweet Auburn recovering after years of decline. Retrieved from http://www.cnn.com/US/9801/17/kings.sweet.auburn/

Pomerantz, G. M. (1996). *Where Peachtree meets Sweet Auburn*. New York: Penguin Books.

Winter, D. (2000–2001). The lost world of Sid and Marty Krofft. In *Keeping and Creating American communities*. (Updated June 2002). Retrieved from http://kcac.kennesaw.edu/thematic_content/building_cities/krofft.html

CHAPTER 10

Building Community Through Performance Activities

Mimi Dyer

In classrooms, performance potentially represents a wide range of activities, from students' sharing responses to guided reading questions, to the creation of original texts based on interpretative analysis. These texts might come in a multitude of genres, including writing, speech, music, construction, and arts and crafts. And because they are so versatile, performance texts may be used across the curriculum. For example, in a high school mathematics course, students might explain how particular theorems could be used to solve equations. In a middle school history class, students might take on the personas of Lewis and Clark as they trek across America. Science students might reenact Alexander Graham Bell's conversation with Mr. Watson, to chronicle the invention of the telephone.

When we wrote the proposal for Keeping and Creating American Communities (KCAC), we incorporated performance as a component for teachers and students to explore. We researched the theories behind this pedagogy and tried them out in our summer institutes. One of the most positive by-products of this incorporation was the close learning community that the KCAC participants established—we became coexplorers of an approach that was new to us, and while we were timid at first, we very soon discovered the power of performance on a variety of levels. We discovered that performance helps build community, and the closer we became, the more we were willing to engage in performance activities. We also built community by studying communities—how they are defined, what they choose to preserve, and how they form and reform. While I had experimented with performance activities previously in my classroom, through KCAC I became enthused about combining them with a community studies approach to curriculum.

Marvin Carlson (1996) believes that "performers and audience alike accept that a primary function of this activity is precisely cultural and social metacommentary, the exploration of self and other, of the world as experienced, and of alternative possibilities" (p. 196). In other words, performances reflect the society that is involved in their production. During the past several years, I have observed exactly that: Performance activities reflect the values of our classroom and in turn help strengthen that community.

In 2000, I was appointed English department chair at Kennesaw Mountain High School (KMHS), a brand-new facility that opened that year with 2,500 students and that was located on 79 lush, rolling acres in the northwest Georgia suburbs. KMHS serves predominantly White, middle-class and upper-middle-class students who live in nearby subdivisions or who are selected competitively to participate in its math, science, and technology magnet program. Working as department chair at this new school allowed me to become acutely familiar with state and county curriculum requirements, at the same time that my role as codirector of KCAC was giving me special insight into the learner goals and principles of that project. So the 2000–2001 and 2001–2 school years provided perfect opportunities for classroom inquiry. The results of this 2-year experiment were definitive: By studying community and incorporating performance activities, my students and I built a collaborative classroom that enhanced students' understanding of how other, often larger, communities function.

The infusion of performance into the curriculum was progressive in that each set of activities built upon the students' experiences in the previous level. We began with classroom sharing based on writing prompts, then moved to interpretive exercises that included letters, projects, and adaptations. All activities were created for ninth-grade honors students in a specially designed course that paired English with Introduction to Technology in a team-taught environment within the Advanced Mathematics, Science and Technology Academy, a school-within-a-school in the larger host school.

CLASSROOM SHARING: ARTIFACTS AND
CURRICULUM-BASED WRITING

I think most teachers include some kind of sharing in their classrooms, whether in response to a question or as a more formal recitation of written work. In light of my KCAC study of performance, I examined my teaching practices and realized that I had engaged students for years with these kinds of activities before I could put a name to them—performance. In its most basic context, a simple sharing is the beginning of incorporating performance texts into the curriculum.

Before I assigned the first task of this nature in my classroom, I laid the groundwork for the sharing process. I told the students that they would be asked to read aloud either a part or all of their response and that they would not be allowed to paraphrase or summarize. I also emphasized the requirement for listening attentively and respectfully to one another's pieces. By providing the rules ahead of time, I let my students know that every voice would be valued. As Lil Brannon says in *Writers Writing*, "By writing, reading what they have written, and hearing the response of readers, students see that writing is genuine communication. They are no longer giving back information to a teacher who already knows the answers, but are finding and conveying their own meanings to readers who are genuinely interested in what they have to say" (Brannon, Knight, & Neverow-Turk, p. 169). Thus, while building the scaffolding for performance texts, I was also building the foundation for a collaborative learning community.

Lucy Calkins (1994) tells us, "A sense of community begins during the earliest days of the school year" (p. 146). So I began the year by asking students to bring in an artifact from home that represented a piece of their personality. They wrote a short description of it, explaining its significance to their lives, and shared the writing with the class, following the above guidelines—a high school version of "show and tell."

From this simple exercise, students began to move toward the goal of forming a collaborative community in which each voice was respected and valued. Some of the artifacts included pictures of their houses or family members, their favorite stuffed animal, a memorable children's book, their first report card, their family tree or crest, and a childhood drawing or piece of writing. Whatever the artifact, students described them with fondness and nostalgia, revealing part of themselves to the rest of the fledgling community. Some students commented that they had discovered things about friends that they had never known before. Drawing on KCAC principles, we talked about how artifacts represent integral parts of a community's heritage and noted that communities are sometimes judged by what they choose to preserve both for themselves and for future generations.

I followed this initial sharing by assigning writing prompts or journal entries based on a piece of literature that centered on community values. The prompts did not ask plot-related questions; rather, they challenged students to look beyond the literary surface to consider character motivation, thematic application, or relevance to their own lives.

For example, in "By Any Other Name," the author Santha Rama Rau (1997), of Indian descent, recounts incidents from when she and her sister were in an English school in colonial India in the 1930s. The headmistress decided that she wanted the girls to have names more pleasing to the English ear, so Santha became Cynthia and Premila became Pamela. As a way of encouraging the class to confront the cross-cultural oppression involved in the headmistress's erasure of the girls' names, I asked my students to find out how their parents selected their names and to write about how they felt about their names and what it would be like if someone suddenly took them away. This activity accomplished two goals: (a) it encouraged dialogues between teenagers and their parents, thus strengthening their home communities; and (b) it brought students closer together in the classroom through the sharing of personal stories, thus strengthening our classroom community. We learned that some names were bound by family traditions and that others were chosen by whimsy, for example, the name given to Seneca, whose mother was particularly fond of that brand of orange juice during her pregnancy.

Because collaboration involves *all* members of the classroom community, when I asked my class to write, I wrote with them; when I asked them to share, I offered to go first; when I asked them to reveal parts of themselves, I did it, too. When they saw that I was willing to peel back the outside layer, they were more willing to do the same. We followed Richard Gebhardt's (1980) advice: "Since students feel fear and frustration privately, they need to be helped to see that they are not alone, that they can receive feedback from others who themselves are fearful and frustrated and so themselves need help" (p. 71).

Today most anthologies acknowledge the importance of journal writing and interpretive analysis, but it is up to the teacher to take the time during class to allow students to share their responses. I found that if the sole audience for student writing is the teacher, students see the task as a chore, another dreaded homework assignment. But when they are encouraged and allowed to share their responses, the audience becomes their peers, and their writing is valued as worthy of performance.

With large classes, sharing can take an inordinate amount of time, so I didn't have everyone share everything every time. Some days I asked students to highlight the most important sentence in the response to read aloud. Other days I called on selected students to participate, thereby establishing a rotating basis. This method also allowed those who didn't feel comfortable on a given day to pass.

INTERPRETIVE EXERCISES: LETTERS, PROJECTS, AND ADAPTATIONS

The series of activities that followed involved more than simple sharing or response to writing prompts; rather, I asked students to interpret texts by projecting themselves into other times and places and creating performance texts from those experiences. Also rooted in community study, these occasions provided some of the most memorable classroom moments of my entire teaching career.

As part of our ongoing practice, KCAC participants search for seminal moments of upheaval that bring about change in the American fabric. None in recent history provided more upheaval than September 11, 2001. For many, this day became a defining moment of change—a time when people asked themselves hard questions about beliefs, traditions, duty, and differences. I, like many teachers, did nothing explicit for a week or so because I didn't really know *what* to do. Then I came to realize that as much as I needed to "talk" with my students about this terrible tragedy, they also needed to talk with me. So I went back to the KCAC belief that "local communities continually redefine themselves in relation to national and sometimes international communities" (Guiding Principles, 2000–2001). And there I had the answer to how we could discuss the issue. I defined for them the conflicts between the Arabs and Israelis, which began with Abraham, Sarah, Hagar, Isaac, and Ishmael, and how decisions made thousands of years ago have affected international—and thus American—communities today.

For this lesson, I combined three of KCAC's core strategies: the restorative and generative nature of writing, the power of images, and the strength of student performance. Because we know that one way students learn to become critical thinkers is by engaging in activities that are relevant to their lives, I challenged them to remember what they were doing when the airliners crashed into the Twin Towers and the Pentagon. And I asked them to find an image depicting events of September 11 or afterward and to write a letter to their future grandchildren, explaining the image and why they chose to preserve it for them. What emerged were heartfelt messages from one generation to another, cajoling, imploring, remonstrating, and demanding remembrance of this day. They became makers of literature by creating artifacts for future generations. Their letters were powerful reflections on September 11. Some focused on the attacks themselves, chronicling exactly what happened; some addressed the lives lost and the ramifications for families; some became flag-waving patriots committed to rebuilding buildings and lives; and others talked about how it affected them, how they changed because of a single day.

Naturally, there were some who simply completed the assignment without a thought other than doing what I asked them, but there were others who took it seriously and created works that they will truly preserve for their future grandchildren. The "performance" of reading the letters aloud and sharing the images solidified for me the importance of student sharing. One by one, each volunteer stood at the front of the room and read; this time no one demurred; no one clapped in appreciation as we usually did.

It was as if the world stood still while we poured our hearts out, and many of us were moved to tears. This act of sharing brought us together as a classroom community in a way that a prescriptive activity could never do. We looked into one another's souls—we nodded heads, we held hands, we hugged. And as we learned about other cultures, we discovered that while people's appearances may vary, all communities have the same basic tenets, which include respect for others and a belief in a higher entity, and those conclusions helped us to a broader understanding of community.

After our performances, I asked all the class members to reflect in writing on the implications of the assignment, including the performances. As I read their reflections, I realized that they demonstrated my students' intense engagement with the process of writing, selecting an image, and performing:

- "The projects we completed were useful for the healing process after this tragedy. We had a chance to really look back at the events and think about what happened and how it affected us." (Cashin)
- "After the attacks on September 11, 2001, I was confused about how I really felt about the whole situation and I was not quite sure I fully understood everything that happened. When we did the letter to our grandchildren, it helped me realize what I really felt and to be able to express in written and oral form." (Amanda)
- "While listening to other people tell how they felt about it {September 11}, I realized we all felt angry, scared, and worried for future generations. I realized that the attack was against every American, even me." (Brett)
- "Writing this letter finally allowed me to express my true feelings on this issue. I felt this was a healthy step in beginning the healing process. I began to write down things and emotions that I did not even know were inside me." (Jakina)

The students' reactions to this activity certainly affirm Turner's (1998) assertion that "the actor may come to know himself better through acting or enactment; or one set of human beings may come to know themselves better through observing and/or participating in performances generated and presented by another set of human beings" (p. 81).

As a result of students' efforts in the basic individual interpretive performance model, I knew that they were ready to become involved in a more complicated community/performance activity, one that involved cross-curricular collaboration of both students and teachers. Carlson (1996) reinforces Calkins's theory when he suggests, "Performance is experienced by an individual who is also part of a group, so that social relations are built into the experience itself" (p. 198). Understanding this symbiotic relationship between collaborative community and performance helped when we began cross-curricular learning with Homer Hickam's (1998) *October Sky*, a novel that was later made into a major motion picture.

Using our community lens, we read Homer "Sonny" Hickam's autobiographical novel about a boy's dream of escaping the coal-mining hills of West Virginia and becoming a NASA engineer. The novel, interestingly subtitled *A Memoir*, became our case study of teamwork and community involvement. Students saw immediately that there would have been no achievements for the Rocket Boys without the help of community members. So when it came time for our culminating performance activity, I called upon the physics, chemistry, and technology teachers at my school. I charged the students to help these teachers (who had not read the book) to interpret the text so that they could assist in re-creating the kinds of rockets that Hickam and his friends manufactured in the story.

I agree with Richard Schechner when he says, "Performance is a mode of behavior, an approach to experience; it is play, sport, aesthetics, popular entertainments, experimental theater, and more" (quoted in Turner, 1998, p. 4). So I planned performance activities that entailed both rocket construction and speeches delivered prior to the launch. Together, students and teachers experimented with rocket candy as fuel; they learned about lift, drag, and trajectory; and in teams, they built rockets—just like the protagonists. They worked together as cross-curricular learning communities, including both students and teachers, to ensure that their rockets would function properly. In their speeches they described the challenges and triumphs of construction and of working in teams to achieve a successful launch, just as Sonny had done when he took his rockets to the state science fair. And, as in life, there were successes and failures: Some rockets were successful, and some didn't make it off the launch pad.

But the process that the students went through was worth all the effort. Because our work paralleled the novel, students gained a better appreciation of rocket building and the emotional roller coaster that the main character endured in his undaunted search for achievement in rocketry. Students were also able to understand firsthand how the small community in which Sonny lived provided the support and expertise for the boys' success and how the performance task of building, launching rockets, and analyzing the process through speeches simulated what Sonny and his friends experienced.

Having successfully negotiated the rough waters of cross-curricular performance collaboration, students appeared eager for the following level, which involved an interpretive adaptation of a drama. *Romeo and Juliet* is required reading for all ninth graders in our state, so I included it in my syllabus, but this time my students and I applied our community lens to Shakespeare's timeless tragedy.

We looked at how the communities of 13th-century Verona, including the Capulets and the Montagues, the prince and his entourage, the servants, and the clergy, contributed to the tragic conclusion for the lovers. We learned from our study that, unlike the helpful community in *October* Sky, some communities do not provide positive reinforcement for their members. Indeed, in this case, all the participating communities were collectively responsible for the ultimate deaths of six of their members.

The students, even though they knew the ending of the play, deep down wanted something to happen so that the lovers would miraculously be together in a fairy-tale ending. But what they learned instead was that families and communities don't always act in the best interests of others; sometimes they are selfish and interested in only what the community has to offer them. They learned that Romeo and Juliet's fate was not simply rooted in the hands of the lovers themselves; it was also constructed by the self-centered carelessness of those who professed to love them.

Advocating his approach, Turner (1998) writes in *The Anthropology of Performance*, "A drama is never really complete, as its etymology suggests, until it is performed, that is, acted on some kind of a stage before an audience. A theatrical audience sees the material of real life presented in meaningful form" (p. 27). Continuing to combine the elements of community and performance, as a culminating activity for *Romeo and Juliet*, students, in groups of three or four, chose a scene for adaptation. I charged them to demonstrate how one of the several communities influenced the plot. The requirements included selecting a new setting, rewriting the script to reflect the dialect for the chosen setting, utilizing at least some costuming, and incorporating music that was appropriate to the designated setting and tone. They then memorized their lines and performed the creations for other ninth-grade classes.

Not unexpectedly (after all, these were ninth graders), several groups chose act 1, scene 2, the "fight" scene between the Capulet and Montague servants. One group set the scene in 1940s Chicago (see Figure 10.1) and used the prologue to *West Side Story*. The dialogue reflected the Mafia era but maintained the integrity of Shakespeare's original script. Vincent commented, "I think that these skits gave us a chance to expand our understanding of *Romeo and Juliet* in different ways. With resetting the play in different time periods, it made sure that we really understood the basis of the play. Also, working with different people was fun, and it brought us closer together as a classroom community."

Another group chose the same scene yet staged it as a fight between contemporary "boy bands" N'Sync and Eminem and his group. They used music from the bands and wrote the dialogue as a rap that incorporated dance and a simulated fistfight. In her reflection of the project, Gaetana offered, "It was a good way to develop our creativity and group skills. Activities that involve writing and acting make education purposeful and fun at the same time. Also, I got to know a couple of my classmates a little better than before." And many students said that watching different groups perform the same scene helped them understand the play better.

Other adaptations included the television programs *Seinfeld* and *Whose Line Is It, Anyway?*, the movies *Grease* and *Star Wars*, and the historic events of the Holocaust and Pearl Harbor. All agreed that the learning experience and the opportunity to write and perform collaboratively both challenged and rewarded them. John summed up many opinions when he said, "I believe that the restaging of a scene in *Romeo and Juliet* was a good experience for all of us. Restaging and rewriting the scene

Figure 10.1. Montague and Capulet servants as denizens of 1940s Chicago. Left to right, Adam Bolan, Daniel Stensland, Alex Caulk, and Paul Barnhill; seated, Vincent Neri.

and then performing it is a lot more complicated and more difficult than one would imagine. I learned from this that memorizing lines and reciting them at home is different than performing, as an understanding of the scene is required to actually do a good job." John came to realize that in a performance, students must understand the material at the highest level in order to write an original adaptation of a particular scene, and they must have the ability to work cooperatively in order to make the performance successful.

The distance between adaptation and original historical drama didn't seem so great, because of the scaffolding we had established throughout the year. The "Voices of the Trail" performance project came about as a result of our reading Diane Glancy's (1998) *Pushing the Bear*, a novel of the Cherokee removal from Georgia to Oklahoma in the 1830s. Ms. Glancy had come to our KCAC summer institute, so I was eager to see students' reactions to this powerful novel based on the 1,000-mile journey of a betrayed people. As we read, we discussed the power of the Cherokee Nation in terms of its community strength in establishing systems of government and written language and in terms of the support they extended to one another during the Removal process. As a culminating activity, I asked the class to summarize four characters' roles in the novel. I then asked them to revise one piece for performance, but I wanted them to experience an audience larger than just their peers. I called Hayes Elementary, our feeder school, and spoke with an administrative assistant, who told me that third graders study the Trail of Tears each year. And voilà! I had an audience, and more important, we were going to be involved in community outreach. So I asked students to revise yet again for an audience of third graders, and we made sure that each student represented a different character from the novel. We shortened the sentences and looked carefully at all the vocabulary to make sure that it wasn't too difficult for our audience.

The next hurdle was to select a date for the performance. I suggested that the 24 of us go to the elementary school, but the third-grade teachers really wanted a field trip, so they came to us. Well, originally I thought it would be a small group and that we could have them in the small rehearsal theater, since it's so cozy. Little did I know that the *entire* third grade wanted to come—182 of them! So the main theater stage became our only option.

We discussed costuming and staging in class. David Foster (1992) maintains that the key to success in collaborative groups is to "cede to those groups as much autonomous authority as possible within the framework of the course organization" (p. 203), so I let the students make most of the decisions because it was to be their performance. They decided that everyone should wear black pants, shirts, and shoes and that each person could accessorize with a simple piece of extra costuming. Some wore shawls or blankets, some carried baskets, while others added nothing. They also staged the performance by having all the characters walk in a circle (representing the march itself) in silence, with each student breaking away to the microphone when it was his or her turn to speak.

The play went without a hitch. I introduced the drama with historical background, and all 28 members of the class recited their lines with dignity and pride. The third graders were silent throughout the performance and applauded politely at the end. Then we all adjourned to the courtyard for a "meet and greet." For about 15 minutes the third graders asked questions of the big freshmen, including a few about the play, but more about life for them as high school students. We left them awaiting their buses to return to Hayes, having experienced firsthand the power of reaching out to an extended community.

When I read the students' reflections about our performance, I was gratified that we had made the effort, because almost everyone talked about how engaging it was and how much they appreciated the opportunity to do something different. Some even said that it was the first time they had performed on stage and that they actually liked it. The process of researching, writing, and performing the play affirmed the theories that had driven me to re-view the way I approach teaching and learning. The students effectively combined KCAC guiding principles in that they wrote to create community, they collaborated, they engaged in research, they created written texts based on the research, and they demonstrated their knowledge through performing for an external audience.

ANALYSIS AND IMPLICATIONS

Nancy Atwell (1991), in *Side by Side*, writes, "When teachers invite students to become partners in inquiry, to collaborate with them in wondering about what and how students are learning, schools become more thoughtful places" (p. 3). I think that my classroom has become a "more thoughtful place" as a result of my 2-year inquiry. The synthesis of performance and community studies helped create collaborative communities that had positive influences for both my students and my pedagogy.

My students became partners in inquiry and contributed to more thoughtful classroom spaces; they saw themselves as knowledge makers, not just knowledge users. I learned, as Traci Blanchard suggests in her essay for this collection, that the objective of performance texts is not just the product itself but rather the process students undergo in the creation. Additionally, by engaging in these kinds of activities, my students and I established our own performing community that nurtured respect for both individual and collective learning and encouraged everyone to apply strategies and approaches for creating new literatures.

Donald Murray (1985) suggests, "Publication completes the act of writing. . . . There is a new confidence, a new identity. They [the writers] have made something that was not here before; they have spoken in their own voice and they have been heard" (p. 61). In other words, writing makes words *public*. In the activities described above, students studied community cultures and made them public by both writing and performing. They wrote their own texts and went one step further by presenting those texts to both internal and external audiences. And in the process they created their own classroom community that encouraged new ways of learning. Thus, they were involved in both the process of creating community and the product of keeping that community culture alive for themselves and others through performance texts.

I believe that implications for my future teaching are limitless. Based in part on my KCAC involvement, I am no longer a classroom teacher. Instead, I am the coordinator of the Math, Science & Technology Academy, of which my ninth graders were a part. The lessons I learned during my 4-year tenure as KCAC codirector will stand me in good stead for my future work. Already I have presented the activities and theories outlined above to audiences at local schools and professional conferences, and I am confident that, as a result, other teachers will begin to review their curricula through a lens of community studies and will attempt to infuse them with innovative, engaging performance activities.

REFERENCES

Atwell, N. (1991). *Side by side: Essays on teaching to learn*. Portsmouth, NH: Heinemann.

Brannon, L., Knight, M., & Neverow-Turk, V. (1982). *Writers writing*. Montclair, NJ: Boynton/Cook.

Calkins, L. (1994). *The art of teaching writing*. Portsmouth, NH: Heinemann.

Carlson, M. (1996). *Performance: A critical introduction*. London: Routledge.

Foster, D. (1992). *A primer for writing teachers: Theories, theorists, issues, problems* (2nd ed.). Portsmouth, NH: Boynton/Cook.

Gebhardt, R. (1980). Teamwork and feedback: Broadening the base of collaborative writing. *College English 42*, 69–74.

Glancy, D. (1996). *Pushing the bear: A novel of the Trail of Tears*. New York: Harcourt Brace.

Guiding principles. (2000–2001) In *Keeping and Creating American Communities*. Retrieved June 30, 2002 from http://kcac.kennesaw.edu/curricular_ program/guiding_principles/gprinc.html

Hickman, H. (1998). *October sky: A memoir*. New York: Dell.

Murray, D. M. (1985). *A writer teaches writing* (2nd ed). Boston: Houghton Mifflin.

Rau, S. R. (1997). By any other name. In K. Daniel & R. Sime (Eds.), *Elements of literature* (pp. 367–371). Austin, TX: Holt, Rinehart and Winston.

Turner, V. (1998). *The anthropology of performance*. New York: PAJ.

CHAPTER 11

Composing History: Linking Community Stories in a Music-Drama-Documentary

W. Scott Smoot

When students seem uninterested in their own research, their teachers might be heartened to know how one research project became a showbiz phenomenon. Choreographer Michael Bennett recorded 24 interviews with performers in the chorus who had danced their youth away behind Broadway stars, out of the spotlight. He could have transcribed these tapes for an oral history, or analyzed them for a study of why these athletes exert themselves so long for such meager reward. Instead, Bennett worked with one of the dancers, Nicholas Dante, to link the stories in a script (Sheward, 1994, p. 236). After previewing their drama-documentary, they brought in playwright James Kirkwood, composer Marvin Hamlisch, and lyricist Edward Kleban to create a hybrid genre—music-drama-documentary. They called it *A Chorus Line* (Hamlisch & Kleban, 1982).

One harrowing song in it, called "At the Ballet," presents the family stories of three different women dancers. Driven out of their family homes by different emotions, all three find similar comfort in the dance studio and sing the refrain "Everything was beautiful at the ballet" (Hamlisch & Kleban, 1982). But what if Bennett had written a conventional term paper, published an oral history, or produced a book-length study? Would millions have acclaimed his work? Must presenters of history always aim to report facts objectively, or is it valid sometimes to compress and elaborate the source material to make it live in the imaginations of an audience? Is the mediation of songwriters, playwrights, and actors any more problematic than the mediation of historians and editors? Is editing of material by creative artists more problematic than the original sources' own selective memories?

These are not questions that concerned me when I started a show of family stories based on the experiences of my sixth-grade students at The Walker School, a K–12 college-preparatory private institution in Marietta, Georgia. Founded by Episcopal priest Joseph T. Walker at a time when the state legislature was discussing closure of public schools, the Walker School offered a quality alternative to students of all races. Today, the school enrolls around 1,200 students, with proportions reflective of the county's racial mix, about 8% students of color. Initially my students and I were interested only in putting on a good show. I imagined something like *A Chorus Line*: kids on stage, playing composites of their elders, maybe with songs. But even among sixth graders, questions arose about what's real when a true story changes in the telling.

We also discovered an essential connection between writing history, writing songs, and acting. Historians draw comparisons between eras even while they highlight the uniqueness of events, and so we say that "history repeats." In terms of song lyrics, we might say that one time "rhymes" with another, or we might say that each particular story is like the verse of a song, while its resonance to the listener is what the refrain expresses.

Handling primary source material with music and drama in mind, my students found how one generation's unique experience can rhyme with their own. Actors' techniques helped them to imagine living through the events themselves, and thinking like songwriters freed them to mix and match material that was unusual for teachers of social studies and language arts.

Here, then, was a project that illustrated several of the guiding principles of the Keeping and Creating American Communities (KCAC) program. It connected students with families—their own and their friends'—in a cross-generational community. It taught the give-and-take of collaboration, and as the project spanned age groups, it spanned disciplines. It culminated in a performance of story-sharing which we called "The Generations Project."

MUSIC AND DRAMA: AN ALTERNATIVE TO THE RESEARCH PAPER

Before this project, I had taught 20 years of history, research, and writing during school. I had directed drama clubs after school hours. I'd written musical plays about historical eras. But these used music and snappy dialogue as add-ons, imposed on the content for entertainment value. I had not considered how thinking in terms of music and drama might be an organic part of teaching with primary sources, engaging students both in relating to the material and in presenting their learning in a public way.

That changed when I accepted the invitation from KCAC lead teachers to participate in a conference called "Where Research Meets Creativity." I was to stage a play based on students' research into a community. That aim dovetailed with my plans to use real-life family stories in my sixth-grade drama class. My hope was that a dose of reality would give the students' storytelling a depth of character and a narrative logic missing from fantasies and improvs of students in previous semesters.

From the first, I expected to add music to this drama. I had two reasons. First, a quirk in that year's schedule required me to fold the sixth-grade music curriculum into my sixth-grade drama curriculum. Second, I already had some experience using a musical form to shape material that lacks dramatic form. I had assisted the previous year in a similar KCAC conference, "Bridges to Community." There I adapted three girls' essays about learning English as a second language into a play titled *The Language Trio*, which combined elements of a three-movement musical sonata.

For this year's conference, I would have no given text, and I was determined that my students would do the research and writing themselves. With the conference focused on research, I hoped my students might achieve the objectives of a traditional research paper through this hybrid form. Certainly, this music-and-drama class was not the right context to drill students on proper use of quotation marks and MLA citation methods. Nor was it appropriate for them to argue a thesis. But Jennie Nelson's (2001) study of college teachers' practices in assigning research term papers reveals that their highest goals don't concern the form, or even the content. Their objectives, as Nelson explains, include helping students to "become better investigators, conceptualizers, critics, and writers," who "learn higher-order thinking skills that will color the way they receive, process, formulate and communicate ideas the rest of their lives" (p. 3). Nelson's subsequent study of students' actual research experiences and professors' candid assessments shows a great disparity between the goals for assigning term papers and the results in the traditional classroom.

This project had the potential to achieve those highest goals by using a nontraditional approach emphasizing primary research for creative purposes. My students would be "investigators" interviewing relatives during the upcoming spring break. Then they would conceptualize by putting themselves into the times and places of their stories. Using music and drama, they would find relations between stories and find new ways to "process, formulate and communicate" the events, settings, and feelings of past times.

ACTORS' QUESTIONS

We prepared for interviews by role-playing. I took the role of my own grandmother, while students asked questions. I suggested that they ask easy questions at first, to put "Grandmother" at ease. Immediately I discovered that this was insufficient prepping, for their first questions were of the fill-in-the-blank sort, dead ends:

> Q. What's your name?
> A. Harriet.
> Q. Do you have any children? [When classmates pointed out that she obviously had *grandchildren*, this was modified to] How many children do you have?
> A. Three.
> Q. How old are you?
> A. 104.

I broke character to suggest that they ask some questions that would make me want to say more than a few words. It was a hard lesson, though, for the interview that followed was not much better—instead of one-word answers, I got maybe four words.

Before I tried another role-playing exercise, we reflected on what had happened to "Grandmother." I confessed that although I'd only been play-acting, I had felt increasingly frustrated and hurt as they'd quizzed me about names and numbers, never asking for more details. It was as if the answers meant nothing. Speaking for myself as well as for my grandmother, I explained, "We adults long to tell about loved ones and loved places, and to make others understand why we loved them. We want these to live in memory after we're gone." Students took this into consideration and came up with some interview guidelines, which I later realized were consistent with those developed by Brown (1988):

- Ask actors' questions that will make the subject want to tell more: "How did it feel?" and "Why did you do that?"—not, "How many?" or "What date?"
- Ask especially about the subject's own elders, about favorite places, about anxious moments, about how national events impacted their lives.
- Write notes but let the subject write notes, too—so that the interviewer doesn't seem to care more about spelling than listening. Students decided that a tape recorder would be distracting. As Brown (1988) points out, if a recording device is used, it's a good

idea to have a partner watch the equipment while another asks the questions as naturally as possible.

STORIES TRANSFORMED IN THE ACTING

Bringing research alive involved what professional storyteller David Roche (personal communication, February 6, 2002) called "putting us in the moment." In a workshop with my students, he told us to start any story in the middle, to speak in present tense, to avoid *and then we went* and *the next day*, and so on. We had practiced imagining the sensations of a moment and adding mime to make action visible for the audience. Applying these storytellers' tricks to "bring research alive" for an audience required poetic license that I would never allow in an academic essay.

For example, Evan's first draft, for which he interviewed his father, sounded something like this: "When my dad was 12, he was playing baseball, and he hit the ball right into his neighbor's headlight. It was a Porsche! He had to work all summer to pay for it." I coached Evan through reliving the story instead of just telling it. I asked some actor's questions about setting, character, and mood. I reminded Evan that in drama, what happens *to* a character is much less interesting than any decision coming *from* the character. I gave him this starting line: "I *am* my father, 12 years old." Here is the dramatic monologue that resulted, written down following Evan's revised performance for classmates. The directions in brackets describe his performance and were included to help any actor to re-create the monologue:

California! [*Actor swaggers up to center stage, "cool" as can be*] Land of cool cars, surfers, and rich movie stars. I am my dad, age 12, playing in my California neighborhood. It's a nice, sunny day, and we are playing baseball in the cul-de-sac. [*Leaning down to pick up an invisible "bat" as he speaks*] I walk up to the plate and pick up the bat, fingering its rough wooden handle. My friend Pete is pitching. He winds up, and throws the ball. [*Aside*] Now I, being the star player, swing the bat. [*He does swing.*] SMACK! Right on the sweet spot, I can barely feel it. It whizzes past Pete, past Richy in center field . . . SMASH! [*He cringes, retreating a step with each phrase*] into some glass—in a headlight—in my neighbor's car—which happens to be a hopped-up antique—an antique PORSCHE! All my friends crowd around the car. [*As he speaks, he approaches the smashed car with increasing dread*] I walk up slowly behind them. I pick up the ball, looking at the smashed headlight. "Let's get outta here!" says

Pete. "No," I say, "we have to tell them. I don't want this nagging me for the rest of my childhood. All I want to do is to work off this cost, and put all this behind me."

His first story had focused on the headlight; his monologue now focused on a decision to accept responsibility despite a friend's advice. Acting it out with body and voice had given Evan the feel of the bat, the sensation of the hit, the slow walk—details that his father had not transmitted. Then performance brought another surprise. Evan still held an imaginary base-ball when he said, "I wanted to put it all behind me." Naturally, he tossed it behind him. CRASH! We added the sound effect of breaking glass, Evan winced, and we had a tag that earned laughter and applause at our eventual performance for a public audience outside our classroom.

In Savannah's remarkable story, her grandmother, after having received phone notification that her son had died in Vietnam, suffered a collapse, then was paid a visit in the hospital by her son. His death had been misreported! The first draft of the story was long, covering several days, from phone call to hospitalization to visit. For her final draft, Savannah compressed all that action into the moment when the mother awoke in her hospital bed to receive a visitor. As she was acting it out, I asked her to imagine what the character would see and think. Savannah added plausible details on the periphery that helped us to imagine the essential event:

> As I was waking, I saw a pale-faced reporter on a TV above my head: [*With a somber news anchor's voice*] "There have been 700 casualties in Vietnam this month. [*Sudden perky expression.*] And now a message from Pert Shampoo!" I looked around and saw white all around me . . . Then I remembered a phone call . . .

As we saw with Evan, the physical movement and in-the-moment visualization helped the actors to imagine more than they had done just sitting and writing. The need for an actor to know what a character is imagining during speech produced Savannah's impressions of regaining consciousness. Acting is more than writing words, and it can connect a student viscerally to a past moment more than words alone might do.

Students wrote these second drafts as Evan did, specifying stage directions in brackets. These added effective voice and movement to stories. The anecdotes and memories had become monologues, opened up by imagination and physical acting. Still, they didn't hang together, and there was a deadening sameness to many of them. It was time to put that sameness to use in musical form, making repetition an asset.

COMPOSITION WITHOUT MUSIC

Students had each performed three monologues, one about family, and two others. The performances were like first drafts. Now it was time for each student to choose one or more of these pieces to refine in writing, as if for a portfolio. But instead of being gathered into individuals' portfolios, these pieces would be combined into three group shows. The students who chose *The Generations Project* worked with the best family monologues from the whole class, not just with their own six monologues. At the same time, their material on other themes was getting attention from the other groups.

Collaboration meant that they surrendered control over their own stories in the interest of creating these compositions. At first, some students didn't understand how ownership of the pieces and the process had shifted from individual to communal. But they came to enjoy playing with one another's stories and seeing their own performed by others.

I directed the students to use class time to compose their classmates' written monologues in ways that would involve the audience with different emotions. Mime, music, and choral speaking were some of the ways we had practiced that might help them to achieve variety. I also gave the students a form on which to propose a sequence for the stories, adding this note: "If you have combined several stories in a single 'scene,' draw a circle around the ones that are grouped together." At the next class meeting, I was given a list of eight stories; three were labeled "The Military Movement," and the remaining five were "Old Folk Farming" stories.

One student, Jane, kick-started the final stage of writing by providing a model for all my students. She used scissors and a stapler to rearrange bits of stories that had to do with how childhood used to be in small-town America. Her committee read the script aloud, suggested improvements, and gave it back to her so she could write a draft. The following day, she brought back a typed script that, to my delight, used a refrain that gave structure to the hodgepodge of memories. The refrain was nothing elaborate, just a phrase that had appeared twice in Rick's story, that "life was simple." She began with that phrase being spoken by all the actors in unison. Then individuals, their lines short and overlapping one another, told how there weren't shopping malls or fast-food places, and riding your bike to the town square was fun. Several memories concerned how much a child could buy for a quarter, and Jane marked the end of that section with the refrain "Life was simple, life was cheap, life was good!" The next two "verses" concerned kids' games, and chores. The end of each section was marked by the refrain "life was . . ." Just as important, to give the composition variety, the nine actors shifted positions on stage for each "verse." For example, they all bent to work on their "chores" for that section, and they all split apart to various areas to skate, read, or play hide-and-seek for the "games" section.

Another group found these methods too cute for stories that focused on tragedies. They had collected Savannah's story of bad news from Vietnam, a grandfather's story of buying passage to America on the *Titanic*, a mother's story of a tornado that swept her into barbed wire, and Katie's story of a kamikaze attack on her grandfather's warship. This troublesome set of "tragedies" best illustrated how events can "rhyme" when Katie connected the kamikaze attack to the planes that attacked on 9/11. She had visited the World Trade Center a year before the towers fell, and she wrote a brief monologue reliving the visit and reliving her shock seeing them fall. The group asked how they could weave all these unconnected and depressing stories into a single piece. I asked them, "What could you say that comes out of all these stories?" Savannah answered immediately, "Nothing lasts forever." I wrote that line as the first line of a lyric, and asked for a second line. I got "Even towers fall."

Beginning with these two lines, the students fit images from the other stories into a lyric and chose notes for a tune at the piano keyboard, one syllable at a time. Then I used a music-composition program on a computer to digitize the music and to burn it onto a CD so that we could rehearse and perform it with a portable CD player. "Nothing Lasts Forever" brought the entire *Generations* show to a powerful conclusion. The song was the only 2 minutes of actual music in the show. Yet musical thinking had shaped all 20 minutes of *The Generations Project*, giving it clarity of structure, a range of moods, variety in stage movement, and the opportunity for a full chorus line of students to share the spotlight.

SHOWMANSHIP—A PART OF SCHOLARSHIP

Once the writing was complete, the cast had to learn showmanship to get their work out to the public. Much of what we call showmanship is just being attentive to what the audience needs, and it grows with each performance. A shy or inexperienced boy on stage may freeze because he is attending to how he feels, what he sees, what he fears. The showman feels and sees all the same sensations as the inexperienced actor, but focuses instead on communicating a vision to the audience—*it's hot*, or *it's wartime*, or *that actress is a boy*, or *I'm an old man*. Through their several "preview" performances, first in small groups, then for the entire class, and finally for parents and teachers, my students developed a sense of showmanship. They learned to pause for laughs, to make lines and intentions clear even for the people in the back row, to signal them with a final look or a bow when it was OK to applaud, and to keep the audience "in the moment" even when things didn't go as rehearsed.

I observed that the rehearsal part of the process generated more excitement than did researching and writing. In class, the energy level and focus on task went up considerably when we shifted from small groups discussing and writing to small groups acting and jumping around. So I wasn't surprised when one mother, reflecting on the whole project, told me of her son, "I don't really think that the writing and editing were high points for him." This doesn't mean the gathering of family stories or the piecing of them together were forgotten; only that the inner satisfaction of writing is less immediate than the gratifications of performance for a live audience. (See Mimi Dyer's chapter on the power of performance in learning, in this collection.)

After the school year ended, nine self-confident volunteers, including several who had not performed in the original *Generations* show at our school, learned new parts and prepared to perform on a real stage in a large hall for an audience of teachers who did not know them. By now, these young actors were veterans of several rehearsals and previews, and they expressed no anxieties learning new material or new staging to fit the much larger venue.

Audience members were drawn into the stories. There were audible gasps, knowing chuckles, and outright laughter, all at the right places. Those reactions meant that the audience, too, was imaginatively involved in the stories. So there were two kinds of community here. One was the community of "generations" outside the theater, recovered through the students' research process and brought to imaginative life for the 20 minutes of our show. The other was the community of performers and watchers who cooperated in this mutual agreement to believe that Evan was his father, 12 years old, having just learned a life lesson.

Live performance is special this way, but there is a connection between that experience and what we call scholarship. Mixing and matching source material, emphasizing common themes, and imaginatively entering into a real-life moment are necessary for scholars no less than for creators of shows. Our performance at the conference showed that these same exercises of judgment and imagination lie within the grasp of sixth graders.

OTHER PERFORMANCE ALTERNATIVES
TO RESEARCH PAPERS

At the forum following our performance, a teacher who described herself as nonmusical wanted to know how someone like her could replicate our research project. The answer is that musical structure is something apart from notes or instruments. It is the balance of theme and variation, or, in terms of the researched essay, comparing and contrasting.

One familiar form by which a community can express themes and stories without music is the "responsive reading" used in many houses of worship. Psalms were originally sung, and still are in many synagogues and churches, but they are today mostly spoken aloud, alternating parts for a solo reader with parts for the community. Jane used this form when she alternated solo voices with the choral refrain "Life was simple, life was cheap, life was good."

The musical technique of a leader's call followed by a choral response adapts easily to communal storytelling. Spirituals, civic ceremonies that confer citizenship, and pep rallies use this form. To string war memories together, we had a "drill sergeant" to call out questions, and "soldiers" in a line to bark out answers. Some "soldiers" stepped forward to continue stories in a conversational tone, and stepped back in line, yelling, "Sir!"

But music has so much to offer that even nonmusicians may want to find ways to use actual music. Music offers a stage director variety of atmospheric sound, the possibility for dance, a background beat to propel the action, and a natural symbol of community, with its joining of solo voices in the harmony of a refrain. So the nonmusician may search in anthologies of folk songs available in libraries. Students could recast their research in lines that fit the preexisting tune.

Popular culture of the past 20 years does offer some models, too, if teachers have students with musical ability. Besides *A Chorus Line*, available on video, there is Stephen Schwartz's musical *Working* (Schwartz, Faso, et al.), based on oral historian Studs Terkel's (1997) book of the same title, a collection of blue-collar workers' stories in their own words. The creepy music-drama-documentary *Assassins* by Stephen Sondheim and John Weidman (1992) mixes and matches everyone who ever aimed a gun at a U.S. president, enacting the story of each through dialogue or song.

ANALYSIS AND IMPLICATIONS

I plan to build on this project this year, now that my sixth graders will be students in my seventh-grade history class. It gives us a common vocabulary and experience for discussing printed primary sources now. I have always tried to get my students to engage their sources in a question-and-answer, give-and-take sort of way, and to imagine the long-dead authors as real people. I anticipate greater success this year, having students think of their reading as "interviewing," and asking the actors' questions that may lead us deeper into a time period via a single source's mind. I also foresee treating a time period as a "time community," a separate culture, and using musical thinking to compose sources in a new form that will help students to reconceptualize the material. We will, of course, look for "rhymes" between earlier times and our own, and for ways to relate our experiences to those of the characters we encounter through primary and secondary sources. If an actual on-stage performance can result from these exercises, then that will concentrate the experience that much more.

Asked to reflect on her daughter's experience with this project, Jane's mother wrote:

> The generation stories were enlightening and have given Jane a newfound interest in history, which she has always disliked [and] confidence in performing in front of others. Also she gained confidence in her writing skills and her knowledge of editing. She learned that everyone has a story to tell. Jane . . . was very vocal about how excited she was in creating the project with her classmates.

With so much to gain from a musical-dramatic approach to history, why wait for a performance date to try it?

REFERENCES

Brown, C. S. (1988). *Like it was: A complete guide to writing oral history.* New York: Teachers & Writers Collaborative.

Hamlisch, M., & Kleban, E. (1982). *A chorus line.* New York: Hal Leonard Music.

Nelson, J. (2001). The scandalous research paper and exorcising ghosts. In W. Bishop & P. Zemliansky (Eds.), *The subject is research: Processes and practices.* Portsmouth, NH: Boynton/Cook.

Schwartz, S., & Faso, N., et al. (1999). *Working.* New York: Music Theatre International.

Sheward, D. (1994). *It's a hit: The back stage book of longest-running Broadway shows 1884 to the present.* New York: Watson-Guptil.

Sondheim, S., & Weidman, J. (1992). *Assassins.* New York: Music Theatre International.

Terkel, S. (1997). *Working: People talk about what they do all day and how they feel about what they do.* New York: New Press.

CHAPTER 12

History Happened Here: Engaging Communities of Students and Teachers

Peggy Corbett

Much like kudzu, an Asian interloper in the southern U.S. landscape that grows an incredible 12 inches a day, urban sprawl threatens our way of life in Cherokee County, Georgia. Familiar sites disappear underneath the vines' lush foliage, not to be seen again until frost withers the carpet—or, in our case, the landscape disappears under bulldozers and strip malls. Kudzu makes an appropriate metaphor for urban sprawl in its march across much of the United States. In *Bowling Alone*, Robert Putnam (2000) links this creeping sprawl to a number of community ills, including disengagement caused by time spent commuting, increased social segregation along class and race lines, and disruption of community boundaries.

While Putnam admits that sprawl is not the only cause of decreased community spirit, he maintains that it contributes to a national tendency toward civic disengagement (p. 215). Sequoyah High School, with 1,400 students, serves the kind of diverse, dispersed population Putnam describes. Students come from agricultural families with generational ties to Cherokee County, from professional families of metro Atlanta commuters, and from families who live and work in the community but who are transplants from other locations. In a typical classroom I might have several sets of cousins who live within shouting distance of one another and whose parents, grandparents, and great-grandparents have lived within 10 miles of the same place for 100 years; and then I might also have students who live in a golf or tennis community and are lucky if they know their neighbors on either side. Illustrating Putnam's observations, the challenge I faced in Keeping and Creating American Communities (KCAC) at my school was how to address this concept of community with such a diverse group of students.

Yet great change, dynamic inquiry, and exciting products resulted when my students agreed to join me in an exploration of our community. Maps and an index for a pre–Civil War African American cemetery, a documentary video, a grassroots movement to save a historic structure, and a school archive all grew from our initial, tentative efforts to ask questions about where we live and how it got to be that way. The discovery process was at times frustrating, but there was always a sense that we were doing something significant.

As a result of a National Writing Project mini-grant, in 1999–2000 I had already begun experimenting with community studies with several groups of sophomores. Those students investigated social forces that had historically been in operation and the resulting changes, as well as current forces at work and their immediate impact on their community. This unifying theme echoed the KCAC principle that community is a dynamic place formed and reformed and yet uniquely personal. In reflecting at the project's conclusion, the students agreed that researching topics in their community of personal interest enhanced their learning. But although the final products were interesting, the meaningful connections with community were missing. It was enough, however, to encourage me to pursue the methods further.

Joining the KCAC team in the summer of 2000 was pivotal in helping me see the larger connections that were not being made in my earlier approach. I began a process of personal learning that would carry over into my classroom. My seniors finally understood the connections when I grounded the majority of my literature instruction in examining the concept of community and the students' place in it.

A significant issue for me was to find a way to invite my students into the inquiry process rather than to direct them there. Sprawl is a topic that my students understood, and it would eventually provide our entry point into an examination of our changing community. Thus, during the first weeks of the 2000 school year, I explained KCAC principles to my students, the nature of my own teacher research during the prior summer, and my plan for us to identify a facet of community that we might research. My original "planned" topic was a look at the impact of agriculture on our county during the 19th century, which is what my own research had encompassed. As an introduction, we read articles on agriculture in Cherokee County and selected excerpts from Jimmy Carter's (2000) *An Hour*

Before Daylight and Raymond Andrews's (1990) *The Last Radio Baby*. Obviously, we studied these excerpts in a literary light, but I continued to put the community spin on discussion, to no avail—at first. What I recognize in retrospect is that the history of a rural America is almost as remote to students today as the Roman civilization. It doesn't matter to them because they haven't seen it; it belongs to past generations. I had to find a way to illustrate its significance to them.

It was important to me that the students make the initial move toward inquiry. My primary guiding principle, which emerges from the KCAC model, is that students must develop their own questions and assume ownership of their inquiry if the process is to be a meaningful one. While my inquiry the previous summer centered on Cherokee County's rural past, my students stubbornly insisted that the agricultural issues I raised were irrelevant to their current situation. My interest in the Cultivating Homelands strand grew out of my own rural experience and out of my 15-year observation of the erosion of Cherokee County's rural lifestyle and landscapes. My students, however, had experienced the changes with a less broad view. Until they witnessed the destruction of a nearby familiar site, they hadn't registered what was being lost to new video-rental stores and nail salons and ultimately, they discovered, to life as they had known it—and taken for granted.

This was the seminal moment in our exploration: the moment when they began to conceptualize the value in preserving at least the meanings of these places in the life of the community. Ultimately their interest in the rural past evolved from their focus on the changes taking place around them. This anecdote reveals the importance of flexibility and observation. It is necessary to attend to what is taking place around you and to discuss these events from a civic perspective in order to facilitate student interest and its relevance to their lives. Their passion would come later.

Sprawl was at our doorstep. Only a few months earlier, a familiar barn and the old Boy Scout hut at the four-way stop signs near the school had been razed to make way for a new supermarket and strip shopping center. Soon after, the four-way stop signs were replaced by a traffic light, the gas station was sold to an antiques dealer, and turn lanes were added to the highway. Life was changing. The only familiar thing left on the corner was the Worley-Quarles house, an antebellum farmhouse that had stood in sad disrepair for a number of years. During an initially uneventful class discussion, one of the students innocently asked what would become of the house, and I casually replied that it would probably be torn down to make way for a proposed drugstore and shopping area. The students were outraged. Our discussion led us to a point of agreeing that in spite of what was being physically lost in Hickory Flat, there were valuable stories to be captured that would preserve the memory of places like the farmhouse. We were on our way!

Discussion of the encroachment into our neighborhoods, the physical changes taking place, and the social mores associated with suburban culture were the sparks I needed for a natural segue into examining our community. My students and I discovered together the value of recording what we had and had taken for granted before it disappeared beneath the grinding construction equipment. What began as a simple attempt to preserve the stories of those who had witnessed life in agricultural Hickory Flat grew into a passionate project that resulted in a documentary film and a grassroots effort to save a local landmark. This passion spilled over into our everyday classroom activity. When I recall what my classroom looked like that year, I see a kind of literacy that created a purposeful learning space: students huddled in groups working on letters, sprawled on the floor working on story boards, gathered around a computer checking for e-mails from community members, and at my desk with me working and reworking a letter to a government agency begging for money. All were engaged in writing activities that encouraged the development of a classroom community, with community operating in its truest sense of shared values.

Trying to understand the forces operating around the Worley-Quarles house, the students invited the president of the local historical society to visit their class. From Mr. Roberts they discovered that the house was built in the 1830s; that a former slave named Razz Worley lived there until he died and was buried in the Worley cemetery plot across the road; and that the township of Hickory Flat had been a center of commerce for the farming community it anchored. Then they innocently asked Mr. Roberts if there wasn't something that could be done to save the house. Before the interview ended, they had formulated a plan with him to produce a documentary film chronicling the house and its history as a marketing tool to generate preservation interest.

Four months later, the students invited the community to view their documentary at the Hickory Flat Public Library. And the community came, including the real estate developer who had planned to demolish the house. Before the night ended, the Hickory Flat Preservation Committee was chartered, and the developer agreed to work with the group to ensure that the house would not be razed. As I looked around the room that night at students who had come to share their work with the community, I knew it was significant that they were there. The meeting had not been a course requirement and their attendance did not affect their grade. They were there because they were invested in the work; they cared about the product and the outcome in a way that was not evident when they did traditional school projects. They were there because they were concerned for the well-being of their community, and they believed in the value of the work. At the time of this writing, almost 2 years later, the house is still standing, and there is some assurance that it will either be incorporated into the development or relocated to a nearby farm.

Another interesting project with a similar process came out of a different senior class's discussion of abandoned structures and their untold stories. Using a newspaper article I had clipped a few months before that detailed a local lawsuit over the removal of an "allegedly" abandoned African American cemetery, I found my point of entry with another group. Their spirit of moral outrage set this group on a mission to capture the stories of those buried in the historic Hickory Log Cemetery and resulted in a bond with the African American Methodist church associated with the site. These students spent their senior year cleaning, digging, and uncovering buried tombstones; developing a computer-generated map and index of the cemetery; and installing an identifying stone in the graveyard. Along the way, they joined Wednesday-night fellowship, in order to interview family members of those buried there, and attended Sunday services. The process from suspicion to acceptance was a wonderful one, since the church members initially wondered why a group of White teenagers would care about their graveyard.

The church deacons grudgingly agreed to allow the students to work in the cemetery as long as church members were present to supervise. So we began our work one fall Saturday. Students showed up with tools and equipment, and for most of the day they filled bags with trash and raked mountains of leaves. They pulled weeds, dug out grass that obscured markers, and piled junk. Saturday after Saturday the church members watched these teenagers happily working. Then the church members joined the teenagers, and in that spirit, conversations began and relationships were forged. Once again, attendance at these Saturday workdays was not a requirement. Because the students had a choice in the nature of their project, however, they accepted that Saturday work would be necessary, to get the job done.

Together, both groups recovered stories of places and people in an effort to acknowledge and honor their existence and as a means of understanding where we're from and what that means. At the end of the year, the students, with the community's help, had worked as archaeologists, genealogists, and oral historians and created a document that has tremendous historical significance to the church and the local historical society. I will always remember their excitement the day they dug with their hands to uncover a concealed marker and the surprise and delight of church members, who were relieved to finally know the location of the missing grave. In the process, my students engaged with an existing community and helped create a new one.

Several months after the project was officially finished, a group of the students gathered one last time at the cemetery to participate in a memorial service. Through a fashion show fund-raiser, the 21 students raised the funds to finally commission a marker designating the cemetery. This single event demonstrates the level to which the students were invested in their work.

MAKING CONNECTIONS IN THE SCHOOL COMMUNITY

Work like this doesn't take place in a vacuum. My colleagues at Sequoyah High School were aware that I was doing something out of the ordinary and were naturally curious. Many were also very helpful. Teachers participated in the taping of the audio part of the Hickory Flat documentary, accepting character roles, assisting my students with video and audio equipment, and helping my students in the necessary networking to locate interview subjects and suggest guest speakers. They listened throughout the year as I whined, rejoiced, vented, and begged for help.

They also asked questions, and thus I found excellent interdisciplinary collaboration opportunities that apply the KCAC model. During that first year of community-based experimenting, one of my sophomores wanted to do a research paper on a local reservoir and its impact on our community. Collaboration with his biology teacher resulted in an excellent project that examined significant sociological and environmental issues and still met the research-paper requirements of our 10th-grade English and honors science curriculum. Later, one of the English teachers on the faculty asked me for pointers on how to do community-based research on a smaller scale, and in my spare time I met with him and shared resources that might help. I was impressed with the quality of his students' work on topical projects such as church histories, watershed areas, new highway projects, and cemetery research. I was also encouraged in reading their reflections and discovering that they, too, were recognizing the value of their community.

Still later, in my new position in the professional development office as a teacher on special assignment, I received a phone call from sociology teacher Maria Baldwin, a good friend and former colleague at Sequoyah, who wanted to talk about an idea she had for a community-based learning project. I agreed to meet with her at the school, partly because I was still missing the lunchroom, but mainly because I was curious about how she envisioned doing community-based learning with a sociology class.

Maria and I had shared lunch for 10 years, so she was often the sounding board as I worked my way through the ins and outs of developing the KCAC model in my own classroom. Although I had often suggested to other English teachers and to history teachers the advantages of community studies, I had never considered its role in sociology, government, math, psychology, and other disciplines. Maria, however, had been listening, watching, and thinking about how she might find a way to elicit from her students the same level of enthusiasm she had witnessed in my students.

Thomas Guskey (2000) presents an alternative model for professional development, illustrating that changes in teacher attitudes and beliefs result after teachers see evidence of improvements in student learning. He concedes that these changes "come after a change in teaching practice" but maintains that it is the experience of successful implementation that ultimately shapes their attitudes (p. 139). This is in direct opposition to the traditional professional development approach, which seeks to alter beliefs at the outset. With possible good reason, teachers are notorious "show me" types and approach most professional development situations with some skepticism. Guskey maintains that the only "significant affective change for teachers is evidence of change in the learning outcomes of their students" (p. 139). I believe that Maria and her eventual interest indirectly illustrate this philosophy.

For 3 years, Maria watched me first dabble in community-based learning and later fully immerse my students in this method of inquiry. Along the way she listened to me as I worked my way through dilemmas, helped me establish my local network, provided computer space for my students, and celebrated in our successes. All the while, she observed from a safe distance, processed the principles as I worked through them myself, and reflected on applications in her own discipline. In Maria's case, seeing was believing.

This understanding that Maria was listening and processing without my being aware raises another important issue. In "The Function of Anecdote in Teacher Research," Patricia Lambert Stock (1993) describes the value of "teacher talk" in teacher research. Stock objects to the academic notion that anecdotal data has no value. She insists that it is precisely because it is anecdotal that it has tremendous implications for classroom teachers. Rather than view such data as unquantifiable, Stock suggests that moments of great change occur once teachers begin to interpret the actions and reactions in their classrooms. Anecdotal sharing constitutes this interpretation; as teachers share stories, they recognize elements of the stories as similar to ones they have experienced. "In the particulars they recognize the details of their own teaching circumstances" (p. 186). Stock's final assertion is that shared anecdotes enrich our practice. I think this is precisely what happened in our case, even though Maria and I were not engaged in formal research activities or consciously evaluating or reflecting on student behavior or assessment outcomes. Maria said that it was my students' enthusiasm that first intrigued her about the project. She also noticed the after-school meetings and public announcements to classmates on deadlines and meeting dates and was impressed by the level of student commitment.

Maria's idea for a community-based project focused on the Canton cotton mill, which had supported and defined our town for most of the 20th century. Together we examined the sociology textbook and the Georgia social studies standards and discussed obvious connections of the content to her immediate knowledge of the Canton Textile Company, ranging from child labor practices to union organizations that began in the mid-20th century. Several curricular standards (such as examining and analyzing societal, cultural, and structural influences on human belief and behavior and the societies in which they operate) clearly lent themselves to community-based practices. After much discussion and an examination of available materials, we developed an outline, a time frame, and an evaluation plan.

Maria did not feel completely comfortable with the writing component of the project. A social studies teacher with very little practice in developing, assigning, and evaluating writing activities, she felt that she did not have the skills to adequately teach these components to her students. Other concerns Maria had as she began the process were familiar to me. Maria wrote in her final reflection, "I feared that the interviews would be difficult to arrange; I was afraid too many of the mill workers would be dead or unable to recall details, and I feared that students would not be properly motivated to arrange their interviews." She also dealt with typical management issues such as semester lengths, schedule changes, and student ability levels.

In our case, the composition-skills component was resolved by my being a guest teacher on two occasions: once to teach a class on interviewing and once more to work with students on recrafting their interview transcriptions as narrative texts. Our solution to the composition component demonstrates the benefits of opening up a classroom and making it accessible to those who can contribute to our objectives. For a social studies or science teacher, collaboration with an English teacher who might be interested and able to work in a composition objective is logical. This type of teacher-to-teacher collaboration can only enhance our teaching practices.

Success also depends on a willingness to begin making the contacts and developing the community and professional networks that guarantee needed resources. First, I called the local paper with a request to place a small announcement in its community events section with a descrip-tion of the students' plan and Maria's school e-mail address and phone number as means of contact. She also put her students to work compiling a list of names of people they knew who had had an association with the now-closed mill and asking neighbors, family, or church members for names. In this type of research, the answers cannot be found on a shelf in the library. Footwork, phone work, and networks are crucial to success. The networking process evolved steadily as first one and then another student brought in a contact name. Maria also benefited from the knowl-edge and network of the historical society president who had worked with my classes. This network made it possible for Maria to ensure that each student had an interview subject and that coverage of the topic would not be superficial.

BROADENING COMMUNITY CONNECTIONS:
SHARING THE MODEL

Field trips also illustrate both the need and the benefit of teacher-to-community connection. In Maria's case, traveling to the site of the Can-ton textile mill community was an easy accomplishment. Maria contacted the management company that now owned the mill to schedule a visit. Painstakingly restored in 1999 and recast as a loft-apartment complex, the old cotton mill's downstairs lobby houses a museum of pictures and arti-facts of the mill and is open to the public by appointment. The historical society president agreed to serve as a tour guide of the mill, the village, and points of interest associated with life in the mill village. With this contextual framework, the students were ready to begin their own deeper investigation of this community and how the mill served as its center.

In the act of recovery, new relationships and a sense of community develop out of a shared objective, out of discovery of shared experiences and emotions, and in the recognition of shared values. Both in my case and in Maria's, our students were encouraged to associate with commu-nity members on a genuine level. In the sharing of stories, our students entered into relationships with people who were strangers in the begin-ning but who became coworkers in a process. When my students began their cemetery recovery project, the congregation of the church that over-sees the cemetery met them with suspicion and doubt. By the time they were finished, a community they would otherwise never have encoun-tered had embraced them in a very special way. In the case of Maria's stu-dents, a group of 16- to 18-year-olds scattered out into a community of senior citizens to hear stories of "the good old days." When the process was finished, however, they had gained a new respect for the lives and experiences of these people and a greater appreciation of the dynamic history of their hometown. History had happened here, not just in a textbook.

Maria's students also relied on connections with one another and with the larger community. With a final objective of creating a documentary film detailing the cotton mill's role in their community, the students worked together to see that it was realized. The community loaned Maria and the students dozens of priceless photographs, which they photocopied, sorted, analyzed, and evaluated for their use in the film. A script had to be written from the narratives they produced, and a storyboard needed to be prepared for the videographer. Maria was fortunate to connect with a former student who currently worked as a cameraman for a local television station. He volunteered first to come and work with the students on how to lay out a film but later volunteered to do the editing as well. This community connection resulted in tremendous savings for Maria and additional opportunities for students, who took advantage of the chance to work at the television station helping with the editing. Even though she had received a small mini-grant to fund the project, the only cost Maria actually realized was photocopying pictures and duplication of the master video. This, too, illustrates the value of networking and using community resources. In attempts at a similar video project, other possibilities for assistance might include a local community college film class in search of practical applications, high school video production classes, or another medium altogether, such as live performance. In either case, community enhancement is a natural by-product.

Maria later said that she enjoyed the project very much and that she and her students "met many wonderful and interesting people." She also appreciated the "hands-on activities, along with the reading and writing skills, communication, and other so-called real world skills" that her students developed as a result of the project.

With the completion of the documentary, Maria thought she had come to the end of the Canton cotton mill initiative. However, an earlier collaboration opened still more doors. Steve Jones, a drama teacher at an area high school, took Maria's students' interview transcripts and narratives and helped his drama students recraft them into performance text. And Maria found the performance of her students' research so exhilarating that she is already planning to further develop Steve's approach. She recently met with her principal and the advanced-drama teacher to discuss the possibility of expanding on Steve's students' work this year and making it available to the people of Canton and Cherokee County. This demonstrates what emerges once a teacher removes the barriers of classroom isolation: limitless opportunities to teach in a more dynamic, communal, and revitalizing context—with both students and colleagues.

LEADING OTHER TEACHERS TO COMMUNITY INQUIRY

At the same time I was beginning to work with Maria, I started to get phone calls from other teachers who were interested in discovering what application community studies might have in their own classrooms. Most of the inquiries were from elementary and middle school teachers who taught gifted general education, social studies, science, and language arts.

The knowledge and experience I developed, along with the materials I collected or generated through my KCAC participation, have been an invaluable resource. My bookshelf and file cabinet are filled to capacity with books, notebooks, magazines, newspaper clippings, videos, and countless examples of student work that have been collected and created along the way. While these resources take up much more space than a teacher's manual, their contents are much more engaging than any traditional material I have ever worked with. Additionally, the sum total of the project's accumulation, represented only in part on the KCAC Web site, illustrates the generative nature of teachers' collaborating to explore an idea.

When I get a call, I meet with the teacher and together we determine what the needs are in terms of interest, time, materials, and student level. Together we look at the materials and discuss local network potential and other resources that might be needed. Drawing on my experience with the historical society, I also suggest field trips, discuss the appropriate context for the trip, and provide support for the arrangements. Rarely does the same project description come out of our collaborative planning.

Everyone's needs and circumstances are different, so a one-size-fits-all model is not feasible. Further, one look at the KCAC Web page demonstrates that it is impossible to do everything. The lessons on the Web site can be conducted in a day, week, month, or term; they can also be conducted along thematic lines or by joining thematic strands together when appropriate. Subject, semester schedules, and the amount of effort a teacher is willing to make to develop a resource network are factors that determine these choices. They are not, however, limited by traditional barriers such as grade level or ability level, as the lessons are easily adaptable, even to the extent of how long a unit will be or the degree of technological sophistication that is desired in the final product. In other words, the lesson can be modest or it can be grand, but either way, it can be done.

It is important to note that many of the teachers I visited opted to do weeklong units with a narrow focus. One teacher, for example, took her fifth graders, who were studying the depression, on a walking tour of downtown Woodstock, a community within walking distance of the school. There they visited Dean's Store, now a small museum, where a group of senior men have gathered for several decades to drink coffee and discuss the news every morning. They continue that tradition, and the fifth graders joined the coffee club that morning for a question-and-answer session on what Woodstock was like during the depression. This was an outstanding way for a teacher to bring a textbook subject to life and required little extra work on her part.

ANALYSIS AND IMPLICATIONS

The beauty of this type of research and resource networking is its availability to everyone. While we don't all enjoy the privilege of university libraries, urban civic centers, research centers, and other resources that scholars are known to use, there is a wealth of knowledge in every community. Historical societies, civic organizations, local libraries with heritage rooms, community newspapers hungry for local stories, easily accessible local public sites, and even elderly men who gather for coffee, combined with the tendency of people from small communities to be generous, are a definite advantage to even the smallest and most remote areas.

When I joined the KCAC team in 2000, I was intrigued by the idea of students performing authentic research. Working from the assumption that they would prefer this authenticity to artificial and teacher-directed inquiry models, I was willing to experiment with community-based inquiry, on what I thought would be a small scale. The result, however, was a journey in learning for my students and me that I couldn't have imagined when I embarked on the project. Typically, a learning exercise affects the students in terms of skill mastery and, we hope, in their future success in college and life. Possibly, the impact is only for the duration of the unit or the test. What I had never experienced prior to this project was learning that affected my students profoundly on numerous levels, teaching practices that extended to other classrooms, or school activities that reached beyond the classroom to include the physical and social community in its process and outcomes. My students grew to see themselves as important members of a larger community and participants in the civic process in its many dimensions. I am confident that they have the skills needed to view their world, both local and global, with a critical eye. All these things happened when my students agreed to join forces in exploring their larger community.

Also, working on this project with my co-teacher-researchers helped me learn a great deal about my teaching practices, the research process, time management, and the importance of taking a broad view of a picture. The most important things that have come out of it for me professionally, however, are realizing the benefits of collaboration and the value of sharing ourselves with our colleagues and our community. For the first 11 years of my teaching career, I worked in isolation. Of course, I saw people—in the lunchroom, in the teacher's lounge, in the workroom, and on hall duty. But when the bell rang I retreated to my classroom, closed the door, and taught. Once I took the step to conduct community-based learning, I found the idea of working alone dismal.

My teaching life has been enriched through my connections with drama, art, history, and music teachers, not to mention the community collaborators who contributed to our work. I have experienced how joyful learning, teaching, and growing can be when shared with others, and I have discovered that people are always watching and listening, and that sometimes, they really hear you.

REFERENCES

Andrews, R. (1990). *The last radio baby*. Atlanta: Peachtree.

Carter, J. (2000). *An hour before daylight: Memories of a rural boyhood*. New York: Simon & Schuster.

Guskey, T. R. (2000). *Evaluating professional development*. Thousand Oaks, CA: Corwin Press.

Putnam, R. (2000). *Bowling alone: The collapse and revival of American community*. New York: Simon & Schuster.

Stock, P. L. (1993). The function of anecdote in teacher research. *English Education, 25*, 173–187.

AFTERWORD

Keeping and Creating American Communities: American Studies in Theory and Practice

Cristine Levenduski

In describing the challenges and successes of the Keeping and Creating American Communities (KCAC) project, this volume tells a story of pedagogical adventures for students and teachers alike. Each chapter presents a narrative of innovation, describing the best of what we hope might happen daily in our schools. Each also documents collaboration between classroom and community that gives immediate and obvious relevance to the learning process. These talented and dedicated teachers build communities by making their classes a part of the community and the community a part of their curricula. Education becomes unquestionably public and, in several cases, activist in its orientation.

What may be less overt in these essays is the extent to which each of them is also a narrative of American Studies scholarship at work. Contextualizing these projects and the entire KCAC project within the history and goals of American Studies scholarship provides a methodological and intellectual framework in which to understand the accomplishments of these teacher-scholars, and it offers evidence of the success of American Studies as a field whose practitioners aim to make scholarship relevant to the world beyond the academy.

A glance at the leadership of this project and at the members of its national advisory board will explain the connections between the KCAC program and American Studies as a field of inquiry. Sarah Robbins, who developed the initial vision for this project, is one of the leading figures active in the efforts of the American Studies Association (ASA) to involve secondary school teachers in its conference and in the association, and her own scholarship on 19th-century literature and culture is inherently interdisciplinary and shaped by the work of many scholars trained in American Studies. Three of the teachers involved in the planning process for the KCAC project—Mimi Dyer, Gerri Hajduk, and Dave Winter—have team-taught American Studies classes in Georgia high schools; they and other KCAC teachers, among them Linda Stewart, Leslie Walker, and Peggy Corbett, have been presenters at the ASA's national convention. And finally, most members of the project's advisory board are scholars whose work fits easily under the rubric of American Studies and who regard the ASA as one of their primary professional homes. Randy Bass, Thadious Davis, Paul Lauter, David Scobey, and I are all regular participants in the ASA on a national and regional level, and, indeed, the meetings of this project's board took place each year at the national ASA conference. In addition, each member of the board has spent long hours consulting about the program and collaborating with the participants to shape their individual projects. Each of the board members brought to the KCAC program experience with other initiatives that have sought to make the public and popular implications of American Studies' intellectual work more visible to a wider audience. Not surprisingly, then, the collective American Studies training, experience, and inclination of the project's leaders and advisors provided a strong disciplinary base for the KCAC project.

Woven throughout each of the essays in this collection are examples of American Studies methods, issues, concerns, and values. American Studies provided for this project both a network of resources and a safety net. That is, the existence of an interdisciplinary field of study like American Studies afforded a sanction of sorts for the kinds of scholarly activity the teachers pursued. If the individual teachers were not always thinking in terms of a disciplinary framework for their projects, the field of American Studies provided the project's codirectors, teacher leadership team, and advisory board a ready body of relevant scholarship, a collective experience, and a comfort level with interdisciplinarity from which they could conceptualize their work (Frisch, 2001; Robbins et al., 1998; Rudnick, Smith, Rubin, Goodson, & Siriani, 2002; Sanchez, 2002; Scobey, 2002).

Since its inception in the early decades of the 20th century, practitioners in the field of American Studies have been interested both in the overarching stories of America and in the myths that help us understand who we are and what we want to be as a country. Scholars were initially interested in understanding *the* American story, by which they meant the story that marked American arts and culture as separate from those of England and Europe. They asked in particular what it was that made the "new" world unique and distinct from the "old" world of aristocratic cultures and values. For these scholars, America and, indeed, American Studies were marked by a democratizing tendency. If England and Europe provided us with stories of mansions and cathedrals, lords and bishops, the American story, they argued, belonged to Huck Finn, who governed his life by his desire to escape from the civilizing influence of his Aunt Polly and institutions such as the church.

By the middle of the 20th century, however, world events made it increasingly difficult to understand and study American culture through a unified narrative. If the American story included Huck Finn, it also included the mill girls, the ministers, the miners, the slaves and their masters, and the multiple nations of indigenous people. As literary scholars worked to open up the canon, and as social historians redefined the enterprise of writing history, American Studies scholars turned their attention away from the broad, totalizing national narratives, studying instead the local and the specific: the small towns, the heretofore unknown historical actors, and tangible and material tools of daily life. Work such as that described by Sylvia Martinez and Linda Templeton in this volume taps into this important dimension of American Studies today.

Overall, in fact, this volume combines the best of both the local and the broader narratives. For many of the teachers telling their stories here, the power and drama of pedagogical innovation comes from careful attention to the local and the specific. At the center of these essays is the specific—the cemetery, the photo exhibit, the site of the Cherokee Removal, or the house of a former slave. For many of these teachers and their students, as Leslie Walker has shown here, the KCAC project began with the process of learning to see and identify sites of local importance, sites that are common, drive-by sites that are part of the everyday landscapes, too easily overlooked. They worked first to explore these sites and then to figure out how to place them at the center of intellectual inquiry and public scholarship. Learning what questions can and must be asked, of whom to ask them, and how to interpret the answers was the difficult first step in many of these projects. In almost every case, models of American Studies scholarship could be marshaled to provide guidance (Kammen, 1993; Kilgore, 1997; Mechling, 1997). Drawing on these frameworks, the teachers and their students situated investigations of the local and particular within national and global contexts—asking, for instance, what it means to build a new municipal museum on a site that was formerly home to Cherokee settlements, a history typically erased from these present-day constructions.

As teachers worked to understand a site, artifact, or event, the questions they asked and the information they learned moved from the local and specific to broader, more general observations about American culture and about the politics of culture. Implicit in these projects—indeed, explicit in essays by LeeAnn Lands, Traci Blanchard, and Bonnie Webb—are questions of power similar to those at the center of much of contemporary American Studies scholarship (Kaplan, 2004; Sumida, 2003; Washington, 2004). At every turn, these scholar-teachers and their students negotiated issues of race, class, and gender, as well as broader questions of cultural difference and cultural power, through classroom learning experiences that connected with community life. Their objects of study raise implicit questions about values and expectations that are inextricably linked to power dynamics, intertwined into our communities. Which cultural artifacts are worth preserving and which are not? Which cultural artifacts can be exhibited and at what cost to whom? Who is allowed to make these decisions? And who gets to tell the stories about these artifacts? These are the kinds of questions that university-based American Studies scholars would also ask about the sites, artifacts, and events at the core of this project (Lauter, 2001). They are the concerns that link the KCAC initiative with the larger field of American Studies and the kinds of questions that make the framework of American Studies useful, perhaps essential, to the pedagogical work on social literacy and civic engagement enacted and examined in programs like this one (Lipsitz, 2001).

The classroom-based projects at the center of this collection of essays, like much of the work by contemporary American Studies scholars, are essentially populist in nature. As we see in the essays by Peggy Corbett and Linda Stewart, they capture student interest in part because the objects of study are the materials and experiences of everyday life, as opposed to the artifacts and events of elite culture (Farrell, 1997). Like the students in Corbett's classroom, many American Studies scholars focus on the built environments that are rendered nearly invisible by the routines of daily life, on the personal narratives and oral histories of the ordinary folk, and on the products of popular media. But if the materials are of the people, those that these teachers have their students bring to their inquiry are the methods of serious scholarship. Archival research is central to several of the essays in this collection, as is close reading and analysis. (See, for example, the essays by Patsy Hamby and Linda Templeton.) What is most notable here is the sophistication of the research conducted by the students. Perhaps because of the nature of the inquiry and the familiarity of the object of their study, they are comfortable in developing research tools at a level well beyond those expected of most students at this stage.

Another connection between the KCAC projects described here and the ongoing work of American Studies today is their shared emphasis on the public dimension of scholarship. In the performances staged by Scott Smoot's and Mimi Dyer's young actors, the Web-based publications prepared by Bonnie Webb's museum chroniclers, and the productive connections that many of Linda Stewart's composition students made with the communities they were researching, we see responses to calls in American Studies to make scholarship public—to reach out to what Mark Hulsether (1997) has called "wider publics"—in a variety of ways (p. 133).

As this volume of essays demonstrates, the KCAC program has involved collaboration on multiple levels. As their teachers did in the early phases of the project, students often worked together in research teams, on performances, and in an array of community-building projects. As Sylvia Martinez's, Linda Templeton's, and Peggy Corbett's essays demonstrate, by becoming researchers studying community life *along* with their students, KCAC teachers created both a spirit and specific practices for collaboration in the classroom. They modeled ways in which scholarship can profit from public partnerships—the kind of productive collaborations represented by the teachers' own ongoing interactions with university-based members of KCAC's advisory board, but equally so by the coalitions they built with local historical societies, parents, and other community members. In specific strategies described throughout this volume, as in the KCAC project's overarching vision, we see a clear response to a goal set by Mary Kelley (2000) in her 1999 ASA presidential address: building collaborations to affirm American Studies' long-standing "commitment to the public culture" (p. 14).

On the one hand, then, this collection of essays illustrates ways in which, through collaborations such as this one, American Studies can provide schoolteachers with tools and concepts that give the daily work in their classrooms a distinctly public resonance—a significance that helps make learning relevant and productive for students. On the other hand, for university-based American Studies scholars, this volume embodies an approach for answering calls by several recent presidents of the ASA for scholars to embrace an activist agenda. In that sense, the record of KCAC work provided here exemplifies what George Sanchez (2002) has characterized as "collective engagement with the wide public as intellectuals and academics devoted to the study of the culture and society of the United States in these times" (p. 6). This brand of activist scholarship is consistent with American Studies' tradition of viewing its work as a potential agent for social change. If in the KCAC project, the prime focus of activity has been the classroom, both that site itself and its interactions with the larger culture have been conceived of as publicly significant. In this sense, then, the narratives in this volume offer a window into self-conscious social practices crucial to American Studies today—the kind of enterprises Michael Frisch (2002) has hailed as "committed to linking the academy and the real world as a crucial civic priority" (p. 203).

REFERENCES

Farrell, J. (1997). Some elementary questions for an American cultural studies: Response to Mechling and Kilgore. *American Studies*, 38, 41–48.

Frisch, M. (2001). Prismatics, multivalence, and other riffs on the millennial moment: Presidential address to the American Studies Association, 13 October 2000. *American Quarterly*, 53, 193–231.

Hulsether, M. (1997). Three challenges for the field of American Studies. *American Studies*, 38, 117–146.

Kammen, M. (1993). The problem of American exceptionalism: A reconsideration. *American Quarterly*, 45, 1–43.

Kaplan, A. (2004). Violent belongings and the question of empire today (Presidential address to the American Studies Association, October 17, 2003). *American Quarterly*, 56, 1–18.

Kelley, M. (2000). Taking stands: American studies at century's end: Presidential address to the American Studies Association, October 29, 1999. *American Quarterly*, 52, 1–22.

Kilgore, D. W. D. (1997). Undisciplined multiplicity: The relevance of an American cultural studies. *American Studies*, 38, 31–40.

Lauter, P. (2001). *From Walden Pond to Jurassic Park: Activism, culture, and American studies*. Durham, NC: Duke University Press.

Lipsitz, G. (2001). *American studies in a moment of danger*. Minneapolis: University of Minnesota Press.

Mechling, J. (1997). Some [new] elementary axioms for an American cultur[al] studies. *American Studies*, 38, 9–30.

Robbins, S., Edwards, J., Hajduk, G,. Howard, J., Winter, D, Yow, D., & Zagarell, S. (1998). Linking the secondary schools and the university: American studies as a collaborative public enterprise. *American Quarterly*, 50, 783–808.

Rudnick, L., Smith, J., Rubin, R., Goodson, E., & Siriani, C. (2002). Teaching American identities: A university/secondary collaboration. *American Quarterly*, 54, 255–277.

Sanchez, G. (2002). Working at the crossroads: American studies for the 21st century: Presidential address to the American Studies Association, November 9, 2001. *American Quarterly*, 54, 1–24.

Scobey, D. (2002). Putting the academy in its place. *Places, 14*, 50–55.

Sumida, S. (2003). Where in the world is American studies? Presidential address to the American Studies Association, November 15, 2002. *American Quarterly*, 55, 333–352.

Washington, M. H. (2004). Commentary. From the forum on American (Indian) studies: Can the ASA be an intellectual home? *American Quarterly*, 55, 697–702.

About the Editors and the Contributors

Traci Blanchard is the Webmaster and technology coordinator for Keeping and Creating American Communities. She earned her Master of Arts in Professional Writing from Kennesaw State University in 1999. Currently teaching world literature and Advanced Placement English Language and Composition at Lassiter High School, she also serves as the yearbook sponsor and writing-lab manager. Other Web sites she has designed include a language arts Web site for the Cobb County School District, Lassiter's school Web site, and the Web site of an online literary magazine.

Peggy Corbett, an NWP summer institute fellow in 1998, served Keeping and Creating American Communities as the team leader of the Cultivating Homelands thematic strand. A secondary English teacher in rural Cherokee County, Georgia, for 13 years, Peggy earned her Master of Arts in Professional Writing at Kennesaw State in 2003. Currently a teacher on special assignment for her school district, she assists teachers in developing literacy curriculum, including community studies projects.

Mimi Dyer (Editor) is codirector of Keeping and Creating American Communities and Coordinator of the Advanced Mathematics, Science and Technology Academy at Kennesaw Mountain High School. Mimi is a graduate of the Master of Arts in Professional Writing Program at Kennesaw State. She is currently enrolled in a doctoral program for educational leadership at Nova Southeastern University. A National Board Certified Teacher, Mimi is an active teacher-researcher who regularly presents to regional and national audiences. Her article about anthologizing American literature with students appears in *Making American Literatures*.

Elyse Eidman-Aadahl is the Director of National Programs and Site Development for the NWP at the University of California, Berkeley. A former high school English teacher, she has been both a teacher-participant and a national leader in a range of humanities-based teacher development programs. Her research interests include studying how educators in schools and communities construct, negotiate, and apply learning to teaching.

Patsy Hamby, a teacher-participant in the Keeping and Creating American Communities program, is a language arts teacher at Hiram High School in Paulding County, Georgia, and a part-time faculty member at Kennesaw State University. A graduate of Kennesaw State, Patsy has also completed a Master of Arts degree in Professional Writing from KSU and a Reading Endorsement certification. She has been a Teacher of the Year for her school and is included in *Who's Who Among America's Teachers*.

LeeAnn Lands is assistant professor of history and coordinator of the public history program at Kennesaw State University, where she teaches classes in cultural documentation, historic preservation, and historical memory. Her research focuses on class and racial residential segregation in 20th-century Atlanta. In the Keeping and Creating American Communities project, she has collaborated with university students and schoolteachers to explore ways of using community history projects to increase civic engagement.

Cristine Levenduski, lead evaluator for the Keeping and Creating American Communities project, is associate professor of American studies and American literature at Emory University, where she is currently the senior associate dean of faculty. She earned her PhD in American Studies from the University of Minnesota, and she teaches classes in American Studies history and methods, American culture, and early American literature. Her publications include *Peculiar Power: A Quaker Woman Preacher in 18th-Century America*.

Sylvia Martinez is a member of the Shifting Landscapes, Converging Peoples team for the Keeping and Creating American Communities project. A National Board certified teacher, she is a graduate of Agnes Scott College, where she received her bachelor's degree in English and her Master of Arts in Teaching. She currently teaches Pacesetter English and Advanced Placement Literature and Composition at Campbell High School.

Sarah Robbins (Editor) is the director of the Keeping and Creating American Communities program. She codirected two earlier programs for schoolteachers funded by the National Endowment for the Humanities: Domesticating the Secondary Canon and Making American Literatures. Founding director of the Kennesaw Mountain Writing Project, Sarah has written widely on American culture, American literature, Women's Studies, and literacy studies. Sarah is the author of *Managing Literacy, Mothering America: Women's Narratives on Reading and Writing in the 19th Century*.

W. Scott Smoot received his Master of Arts in Professional Writing at Kennesaw State University in 2001. With the Kennesaw Mountain Writing Project, Scott has served as creative-writer-in-residence for the summer institute, chair of the advisory council, and an advanced institute fellow (leading to publication of an essay in *Voices from the Middle*). His play *Her Yankee Secret* was performed under his direction at The Walker School, where he teaches in the middle school.

Linda Stewart was the Pilot Teacher Coordinator for Keeping and Creating American Communities. She is a full-time instructor at Kennesaw State University, where she teaches world literature and composition courses emphasizing interdisciplinary research. At the University of New Hampshire, Linda earned a Master of Arts in Teaching and a Master of Arts in English Literature, and she taught general and honors composition courses. She has secondary school experience teaching a varied curriculum to student populations ranging from at-risk to honors English students.

Linda Templeton worked primarily with the Cultivating Homelands team for Keeping and Creating American Communities. She is a graduate of Kennesaw State University's English Education program. A fellow in the Making American Literatures project, Linda was also coleader for a local Rural Sites Network initiative of the National Writing Project—a program providing professional development for teachers in schools transitioning from rural to suburban. Currently, she teaches ninth-grade English at Cartersville High School in Cartersville, Georgia.

Leslie Walker worked as Team Leader for the Reclaiming Displaced Heritages theme of Keeping and Creating American Communities. She has taught 9th-, 10th-, and 12th-grade English at Campbell High School in Smyrna, Georgia, since completing her BS in Secondary English Education at Kennesaw State in 1995. Leslie was a 1998 fellow of the Kennesaw Mountain Writing Project's summer institute and a 1999 Advanced Institute fellow. She earned her Master of Arts in Professional Writing from Kennesaw State in 2001.

Bonnie Webb led the Building Cities team for Keeping and Creating American Communities. She has taught social studies, science, and language arts to gifted middle schoolers. She currently works at Cooper Middle School in Austell, Georgia. Bonnie holds a master's degree in Middle Grades Education. She has been involved in the Kennesaw Mountain Writing Project since 1996, serving as Advisory Council chairperson in 2000–2001. Bonnie has received teaching-with-technology grants from the U.S. West Foundation, Media One, and Educating for a Sustainable Future.

Index